Happy Teacher Revolution

Happy Teacher Revolution

The Educator's Roadmap to Claiming & Sustaining Joy

Danna Thomas

JOSSEY-BASS™
A Wiley Brand

Published by John Wiley & Sons, Inc., Hoboken, New Jersey.

Published simultaneously in Canada.

For general information on our other products and services or for technical support, please contact our Customer Care Department within the United States at (800) 762-2974, outside the United States at (317) 572-3993 or fax (317) 572-4002.

Wiley also publishes its books in a variety of electronic formats. Some content that appears in print may not be available in electronic formats. For more information about Wiley products, visit our web site at www.wiley.com.

Library of Congress Cataloging-in-Publication Data is Available

ISBN 9781394195725 (Paperback)
ISBN 9781394195749 (epdf)
ISBN 9781394195732 (epub)

COVER DESIGN: PAUL MCCARTHY
COVER ART: © GETTY IMAGES | YUANYUAN YAN

SKY10069998_031924

This book is dedicated to teachers:

past,
present,
and future.

To the Revolutionaries who so bravely pioneered this global movement, thank you for your vulnerability to commit to the radical act of claiming your own well-being and holding space for others to do the same.

You inspire me every day to keep going and keep fighting for the wholeness and wellness of teachers.

CONTENTS

Visit https://www.wiley.com/go/happyteacherrevolution to access the videos and forms mentioned in this book.

FOREWORD

I choose to disconnect and detach with love.

In January of 2017, I resolved to swear off what had become a soul-sucking habit of daily doom-scrolling and replace that fear and dopamine-driven exercise with the intentional consumption of good news and bright spots, stories elevating everyday kindness, compassion, courage, servant leadership, brave truth-telling, and posttraumatic growth. A few months later, I came across an article in *Education Week* highlighting the now-well-known epidemic of educator burnout. This story was different because it was personal, hopeful, and solution-focused without the invalidating tones of toxic positivity. This story was about Danna Thomas and the beginnings of her grassroots efforts inviting us all to take more compassionate care of ourselves and each other by telling the truth, connecting in our shared struggle and strength, embracing our sense of agency, and choosing how we want to show up in any given moment. This was the story of a responsible revolution in service of equitable student outcomes and human flourishing, and I was hooked.

The following year, on the heels of significant loss in our community, we at Salem-Keizer Public Schools in Salem, Oregon, were awarded an employee wellness grant from OEA Choice Trust. We immediately decided to join Happy Teacher Revolution (HTR) and invite Danna to come train 30 instructional mentors, counselors, and administrators in how to facilitate peer support groups oriented toward providing the time and space to *heal, deal, and be real* about the social-emotional and intellectual demands we all face in schools today. This *coalition of the willing* didn't need to be persuaded that this was necessary work. Like many of us who suffer from bouts of harsh self-criticism, these Salem-Keizer professionals just needed validation, permission, basic resources, and moral support. They were already gifted, whole-human wellness champions fully invested in finding meaningful, low-burden, high-impact strategies to influence school culture. They were already committed to the mindset of not letting what we can't do yet prevent us from doing what we can do now.

Danna's contagious spirit and compelling story of personal and professional struggle, active healing, and posttraumatic growth profoundly resonated with our team, as it has with thousands of educators across the United States and Canada. Her elegant upstream solution to the downstream outcomes of empathic distress and burnout is particularly powerful because it is a veritable marriage of sense and soul. Sense comes from her deep understanding of the well-established research related to toxic stress, primary trauma, indirect trauma, educator burnout, and the complex systems-level variables influencing contemporary public education. Soul is reflected in how Danna honors the perennial wisdom traditions with a reverence for the art and ritual of gathering and holding sacred space for our lived experiences to be shared and for all participants to encounter the affirming power of community.

We started with pilot sites for HTR in 2019, supporting early-career educators, 50 percent of whom usually leave the profession within their first five years, and veteran educators who were particularly impacted by the rapidly escalating behavioral health needs of students today. Anecdotal feedback from educators was exceptionally positive—and worries that these peer support groups might devolve into prolonged venting sessions were alleviated when participants and facilitators quickly adapted to the norms, expectations, and structure of HTR. Little did we know how important it would be for us to build more capacity for nurturing a culture of care prior to March 2020. During the pandemic and ensuing global upheaval, virtual HTR groups and the 12 Choices became a lifeline for dozens of educators, counselors, and administrators.

This project also coincided with what would become the first biannual survey of more than 5,000 district staff on the topics of belonging, well-being, and staff relationships—topics similar to those we started assessing with all of our students in 2018. The anecdotal data continued to reflect educators' profound appreciation for this resource—but now that perceived impact had reliable, valid data to support it. Our pilot sites that continued regular HTR meetings in a virtual format had among the highest overall levels of staff well-being in the district and showed some of the most dramatic improvements in positive and challenging feelings, from early Spring

2020 to late Fall 2020 and beyond. This further validated our belief that multi-tiered systems of support (MTSS) for students *must* be accompanied by multi-tiered systems of support for adult social-emotional learning ("SEL involves evidence-based programs, practices, and policies through which children and adults acquire and apply the knowledge, skills, and attitudes necessary to understand and manage emotions, set and achieve positive goals, feel and show empathy for others, establish and maintain positive relationships, and make responsible decisions.") and well-being. HTR provided us with an effective Tier 1/2 intervention to understand, support, and help retain our precious human resources, and we finally had a data-driven lever and a place to stand for advancing work that centers employee wellness as an essential driver of equitable student outcomes.

I have served for more than 25 years at the intersection of education, mental health, and social-emotional learning as a counselor, teacher, school psychologist, adjunct instructor, and district administrator. During that time I've burned out of two jobs, forgetting to care for myself with the same level of intentionality I aspired to care for others. I felt guilt, shame, and shades of imposter syndrome for not *knowing better*, especially given my training as a helping professional. I can't help but wonder if those episodes of burnout might have been prevented, or if finding joy again might have been easier if peer support groups like Happy Teacher Revolution had been available to me then.

If you've ever struggled to say no without fear of relational repercussions; if you've ever felt guilty for going to the bathroom during the school day, taking more than five minutes for lunch, or not answering all emails within 24 hours; if you often feel emotionally and physically exhausted; if you've felt shame for not being all things to all people, all the time; if you feel like you're in a near-constant state of hustling to prove your worthiness; if you've ever wondered what it might be like to work in a truly collaborative Community of Practice where you can lean into your own sense of agency and self-determination; if you've ever wondered what it might be like to feel seen, heard, and valued at your school, with no strings attached . . . then Danna Thomas is your *person* and HTR is for you!

—Chris Moore, Ed.S.
Director of Mental Health & Social-Emotional Learning
School Psychologist
Salem-Keizer Public Schools, Salem, OR

INTRODUCTION

My journey with the Happy Teacher Revolution Movement began before I was a teacher, before anyone referred to me as Miss Thomas, before I held the responsibility of educating a classroom filled with incredible minds. My story begins when I was still a student myself, a student suffering in silence from severe depression, anxiety, and panic attacks. Not only was I experiencing thoughts of ending my life, but I was expending so much energy pretending like I was "okay" when I really wasn't by hiding my shadow from family and friends. But I couldn't hide from my teachers. I refer to my educators as my emotional first responders who recognized the subtle changes in behavior and compassionately encouraged me to seek treatment and get help. They're the reason why I'm alive today, writing these words, and sharing this very road map to claiming joy. I owe them my life.

After spending nearly a decade as an educator, I recognized both the lack of preparedness and the lack of ongoing support for the emotional demands of the job. I was shocked there was no such thing as a support group for educators, so I decided to create an opportunity for systemic change by organizing support groups through a grassroots network in my community. We called it "Happy Teacher Revolution," and slowly our movement began to take root and spread beyond the city limits of Baltimore.

Over the past ten years, Happy Teacher Revolution has supported hundreds of individuals in leading communities to support themselves and one another by creating the time and space to feel, deal, and be real about the social-emotional demands that they face on the job. We've supported these educators in leading their own support spaces from the West Coast to the East Coast, in rural areas and urban areas, in small schools and massive districts across the United States as well as in Canada, Senegal, Nigeria, Brazil, and Kuwait.

My Why

This book is a necessity. While I don't believe in operating from a sense of scarcity or urgency, I realize as I write this that we need a strong teaching force now more than ever. We are already seeing a reduction in the numbers of people choosing to enter the field, and enrollment in schools of education is down. The effect of educators leaving the field is absolutely immense.

The pandemic of educator burnout existed long before the pandemic of COVID-19. According to a 2022 *EdWeek* survey described in *Forbes* magazine, "a whopping 60% of teachers expressed they were stressed out and many educators are considering leaving for the first time ever or have already left the profession altogether due to stress" (Gomez, 2022). When we apply this research to the teachers in the United States alone, that means that of the 3.2 million current teachers—over 1.9 million estimated teachers—are stressed out . . . which means nearly 31 million children are sitting in the classroom of a stressed-out teacher (National Center for Education Statistics, 2022).

As teachers leave the classroom, we have realized that they are a target market for other employers based on their tenacity, resilience, work ethic, and innovative approaches. Furthermore, social media celebrates individuals who share their stories around leaving the profession, with many posts going viral because so many can relate to hitting an absolute breaking point.

Poor-quality teacher self-care, the lack of systemic change, and the complete ignoring of financial well-being are all topics that folks have been vocal about especially recently, and the voices are only growing.

Here are some of the headlines at the time of this writing:

- "Superficial Self-Care? Stressed-Out Teachers Say No Thanks" (2022)
- "Teachers Are Not OK, Even Though We Need Them to Be" (2021)
- "US Teachers Work More than Teachers in Nearly Every Other Country" (2019)
- "Teachers' Pay Lags Furthest Behind Other Professionals in U.S., Study Finds" (2017)
- "Teachers in America Were Already Facing Collapse. COVID Only Made It Worse" (2022)

- "Violence, Threats, and Harassment Are Taking a Toll on Teachers, Survey Shows" (2022)
- "More than Half of Teachers Are Looking for the Exits, a Poll Says" (2022)
- "Educators Are More Stressed at Work than Average People, Survey Finds" (2017)

There's a common thread through the voices and perspectives of the hundreds of humans who influenced this text, and that is an overwhelming craving for a sense of belonging. This desire of belonging—especially for new teachers who don't know what it's like to *not* be a pandemic or post-pandemic teacher. The mentor teachers I've talked to share that they are less in the space of coaching new teachers around curriculum, intellectual demands, or academic facets of the job but more so supporting the social-emotional lens from a humanistic perspective. They pick up the phone or start a Zoom call with new teachers who are sobbing, craving someone to just listen and connect with.

What does the teacher turnover crisis mean? First of all, it means there are fewer people in a field that is already experiencing historical shortages. Second, it also means that schools will be out of money, as it's expensive to hire teachers, and even more expensive to hire administrators. Third, it means that children will be missing out on an opportunity to have a stronger teacher—research shows that teaching experience is positively associated with student achievement gains throughout much of a teacher's career. Every year that students get a brand-new teacher means that the students are missing out on the benefit of having a veteran teacher. Things are hard for teachers now. But, in truth, things have *always* been hard for teachers. We are at a turning point, which I pray will not become an absolute breaking point.

> *Self-care looks privileged because we think of it as an Instagram feed. Going places, doing things, spending money. But it's not like that. Self-care isn't treating yourself, self-care is taking care of yourself. It's legit to take care of yourself. Love yourself. Accept yourself. It's noticing what you need. It's using your voice to advocate for your needs.*
>
> —Alexis Shepard, former Middle School English Language Arts Teacher, Clemson, South Carolina

In this book, a *new* definition of self-care works alongside systemic change. (See Part V about systemic change.) The enhanced aspects of the book, including its interactive design, videos, and shareable graphics, are designed to be digested in small doses without being overwhelming. Thus, they make well-being seem a little less daunting. The voices amplified in this text draw from teachers' experiences in a wide range of locations, with a wide range of backgrounds and a wide range of experiences in their role. Steeped in mental health research, this is the opposite of a "fluffy" book and posits happiness as truly revolutionary not just to pursue but to claim as your own.

This guide is for you if you hope to restore your passion and your *why* for this work. It was created with you and your colleagues in mind as we collectively crave autonomy now more than ever. We are in the work of supporting the growing minds of the individuals we teach and also in the practice of building relationships (with students and with adults), and we know that the importance around social-emotional learning is only growing. In my decade of work as a national spokeswoman for mental health and well-being awareness for educators, the piece that has translated into financial investment is retention of quality teachers and also quality administration. In the United States alone, before the pandemic, we were spending over $7.3 billion on the constant recruitment and training of new teachers (National Commission on Teaching and America's Future, 2007). Our educators are not a renewable resource, and not only is it financially expensive to train a revolving door of new teachers and new administrators, but the emotional costs are even higher.

This revolutionary text aims to support you, dear reader, in . . .

not just surviving but *thriving,*

not just retaining but *sustaining,*

not just functioning but *flourishing,*

not just identifying problems but *building solutions,*

not just focusing on the deficits but *leveraging the positives,*

not just curating individual meaning but *cultivating collective purpose,*

not just repairing the weaknesses but *amplifying strengths,* not just a singular individual focus but a *collaborative humanistic vision,*

not just fixing what is broken but ***nurturing what is best.***

Buckle up. It's about to be quite an adventure on the road to well-being.

A Momentous Road Trip

As this book was being formed, I realized I wanted to cross off a bucket list item and embark on a personal journey that I have always wanted to do. As I was drafting the very proposal for the book that is in your hands right now, I decided to hop into my tiny red convertible and drive across the United States from Baltimore. And back. Alone.

This was a goal of mine since the day I got into a car accident less than a mile from the school building where I taught. After my car was totaled by a driver who hit my driver's side, I felt obliged to go to work the next day because I knew that it would be hard to find a sub since we had been short staffed already. As my back started to hurt more and more throughout the day, a colleague encouraged me to leave early to get evaluated by a medical professional. As it turns out, I *was* injured. The fact that I had chosen to go to work after the accident was used against me later during arguments by the insurance company not to compensate me for my medical claims. After the insurance company attempted to deny my claims, I realized this was an opportunity to learn the value of prioritizing my well-being unapologetically, and also to encourage others to do the same.

I mapped out the route cross-country based on Happy Teacher Revolution sites and Revolutionaries who had launched support groups within their unique communities across the United States. I also aligned the trip to the lunar calendar so that I was leaving and returning to Baltimore on the full moon and spending the new moon gazing at the beautiful stars in Joshua Tree National Park. Well . . . at least that was the plan for my road map. But, as life so often shows us, even the best-laid plans can go haywire, and a series of unpredictable events led me to the most serendipitous adventure that was even better than my original game plan.

As I made it to the West Coast after about two weeks of traveling across the country and multiple years of not even considering that I could make my dream a reality, my engine light came on. And my big plan to spend the new moon under the stars in Joshua Tree? As it turns out, I was smack dab in the middle of monsoon season and risked getting my car stuck in the sand and trapped for days from potential flooding.

My seemingly perfect adventure hit a few hiccups, but as a result I rerouted. I adjusted the game plan and took a moment to allow the current of the river to flow with ease in the direction that was meant for me. I opened to divine timing, synchronicity, and chose to trust that what is meant for me will present itself and what isn't will be let go. I decided to head north to avoid the monsoons before going east and connected with a fellow entrepreneur and social innovator in Salt Lake City whom I may have never had the chance to meet otherwise. Learning about the work of Project Embrace to repurpose medical equipment and specifically offer support for Indigenous populations during COVID-19 (and beyond) was such an incredible opportunity that I didn't plan in my original road map but suddenly became an absolute highlight of my journey. This unexpected detour on my trip led me to adventures like swimming in a crater, maxing out my car's speed in the Bonneville Salt Flats, and weeping tears of joy as I drove past Moab and crossed into Colorado while witnessing the most vibrant sunset in my rearview mirror as I drove through the Rockies.

These pages were formed over the course of multiple journeys across the country and around the world, meeting hundreds of educators and hearing their unique stories. I stayed in their homes, crashed in their basements, met their children and their families, took time to truly understand the stories and perspectives each of them brought to the table. Their voices are featured throughout these pages, and their hearts beat passionately for the message of the Revolution.

As much as I wish I could tell you that this handbook will be a clear-cut road map to a destination of pure uninterrupted bliss, I'm also so glad that this text won't just give you the easy answer. In fact, you may have even deeper wonderings about yourself as you engage with the concepts I've collected for you (us) here in these pages.

What I've realized in drafting a road map to consider my own well-being and mental health in my role as an educator and for fellow educators is this: Life isn't about only experiencing joy and being immune to the rest of the feelings of a human's spectrum of emotion, and that isn't even the point. The roadmap here is not a linear one and the goal is to feel the fullness of each emotion without censoring ourselves to filter in only joy or bliss.

The personal well-being journey you are about to engage with is unique to you. This book has been a teacher for me, and it'll be a teacher for you too if you choose to participate *with* and *in* this text. There is no single specific narrative for your personal growth, your personal journey, your personal well-being that is already *prescribed.*

So therefore . . . you are the creator of this. The painter. The maker. The sculptor. The one behind the wheel. You are the one blazing that trail, journeying on a path into the unknown. So, know this is also nurturing yourself as the creator. Valuing the creation itself of course but also valuing the process in making. Acknowledging the power of the ART in well-being.

> *You are the author of this story.*

Track data for yourself, starting now, to gather a snapshot of your well-being. This is the beginning of capturing observations, patterns, internal seasons and external observances. Some days may be ones where you share, verbalizing the message to create systemic change. Other days are ones where you upload from your incredibly wise body the learnings of your ancestors. Other moments are ones where you hold the red pen, and your ability to nitpick and edit are actually your superpowers. While others are days of integration, where intentionally doing nothing and choosing rest is the ultimate act of rebellion and pushback on grind culture. It all belongs. *You* belong.

The self-help and self-care industry is exactly that, an industry. It is built on the expectation and doctrine of capitalism that happiness is an achievement and that some sort of a fix exists that is so linearly focused on an archaic pedagogy which ultimately misses the mark. Because, dear reader, there is no end goal that can be achieved, there's no check-the-box type of accomplishment by the end of this book. You will always be working through, working on, and working with the evolution of your personal well-being. There are no prescribed steps, automation, or quick-fix pill to get you to "achieve" happiness. In fact, the entire concept of achieving an endpoint or mastery is a toxic way of considering well-being; the healthier invitation is to consider well-being as an ongoing practice.

Similarly, I argue that there is no such thing as work-life "balance." Rather, I believe in work-life *integration.* How can you integrate, evolve, and collaborate with your own learnings about yourself, ongoing research at large, and the larger context of observations as you continue your own journey? How can you participate with this book and consider your personal evolution not only in your path as an educator but your path as a *person*?

The education system was not designed with your well-being in mind. Let that sink in. The system we are collectively working within was not designed to prioritize the mental and physical well-being of either its teachers or its students. The education system was built to teach workers, not thinkers, and certainly not Revolutionaries.

Mapping our revolutionary road map overview

In Part I, we start with the individual. Rooting into our individual well-being and basic self-care is our foundation, building on safety and sense of belonging; next is competency; and finally is an enlightened "self-actualized" sense of oneself.

After exploring the research and practices of nurturing your personal well-being, Part II offers an integrative approach to embody individual wellness as a means of reflection.

Next in the ripple effect outward is self in relation to others. Self in relation to connections with students, colleagues, leaders, and stakeholders is the focus of Part III. We do not operate in isolation or within a vacuum.

In Part IV, you are invited to embody the information presented around facilitating authentic human connection.

Finally, the larger extension beyond oneself is systemic change covered in Part V: large scale impact, societal reprogramming, and how we can collectively move the needle when it comes to supporting well-being for humanity and the generations long after our own.

There also are repeated sections that discuss similar topics around boundaries, engaging with students, and self-care strategies to integrate into the classroom. Additionally, there are repeated parts for reflecting and integrating holistically through the body in Parts II, IV, and VI. These sensory experiences are deliberately sandwiched between the research- and data-driven parts of the book to offer an embodied approach to your own well-being.

This handbook is a support tool for your own personal well-being and is a reference to continue coming back to as your own learnings evolve and unfold. There may be opportunities for you to process backlogged feelings into your own lived experiences. Even further, there may be acknowledgment bubbling up to the surface of ancestral trauma and experiences of those who have come before you. You may be carrying the emotions of your parents, their parents, and so on.

This resource is based on positive psychology, which is the science that investigates the strengths and factors that allow individuals and communities to thrive. This book is written intentionally with sections ending in *-ing* to note the active, continual practice of the work. It's not either healed or not healed but rather healing. One of the things that came up for me in therapy while creating this book was my tendency to operate in all-or-nothing extremes, which manifests as a result of being a trauma response. The extremist view is something I'm working on personally, recognizing that the metamorphosis magic of a butterfly from a caterpillar is encapsulated by the messy chrysalis in the middle. The "messy middle" is something to consider as you begin and continue on this personal journey, and I'm endlessly grateful to be doing this work alongside you. As is so often shared, healing isn't linear.

To be completely transparent, birthing this book has been a completely transformative experience for me personally. Stepping into this role as "author" created an opportunity for me to reflect on the history of what it means to show up as an educator, on the lack of support and preparedness around teacher mental health and well-being, as well as my own individual experiences of grappling with backlogged processing of some heavy emotions. I am so grateful to be the vessel through which these messages and learnings have been downloaded—or rather uploaded—and I realize I am the messenger and deliverer of this important information collected from hundreds of educators over the course of the last six years. There are countless voices in these pages beyond my own.

It's said that the book we write is the one we so desperately need to read. And, in this case, I will specifically name my imperfection and humanity as I realize that I will be rereading this text and its collection of voices assembled within it for decades to come. I realized when I birthed this book that it was absolutely essential that I did so from a place of well-being myself. Throughout the book you will see coloring pages that feature the 12 Choices, which was adapted from Vicki Davis's *12 Choices to Help You Step Back from Burnout*. I invite you to go through each of these 12 choices as they appear and ask yourself if there is alignment in your life right now. And, for those who don't feel aligned, approach yourself with compassion instead of judgment. There is room for you to create your own choices and your own affirmations, and I invite you to develop your own personal relationship with this text on well-being in whichever way aligns for you. My hope is that you also participate in and with this book, dog-earing pages, underlining, highlighting, and sticky-tabbing over and over again. Or simply open to a random page and trust that it is the knowledge and support you needed to hear in this exact moment today. This text is meant to be participatory, and the vibrancy of color and experience that you add to it is uniquely yours and absolutely unparalleled.

This may be the first education book that you read that may spark interest in pursuing a different passion or adjusting what your goals are professionally. It may be the first professional development text that encourages you actually to rest instead of signing up for more. This may be the first educational resource that gives you permission to claim your well-being as your own, to redefine what sustainability looks like in your role, and invites you to be present in your body instead of numbing out from who you are and how you move through the world. Welcome to the Revolution.

Autonomy

In addition to addressing the unique challenges of teaching today, this book shares opportunities to consider one's own well-being through the lens of six different well-being principles inspired and developed by Dr. Carol D. Ryff and colleagues. You have a unique opportunity to check in with yourself and consider your own personal wellness in terms of autonomy, environmental mastery (management of surroundings), personal growth, positive relations with others, purpose in life, and self-acceptance. You'll find a visual representation of each of these six well-being principles at the end of this introduction as well as throughout the entirety of the book.

Environmental Mastery

Personal Growth

Self-care is unique for every individual. Self-care strategies may sound, feel, and look different for a preschool teacher in an urban setting compared to a secondary teacher in a rural setting compared to a middle school teacher in a virtual setting. In the creation of this very book as a resource for educators, I have intentionally cultivated a diverse group of perspectives. This collection of voices is amplified through highlighted quotes as well as multimedia features like videos made accessible through QR codes and digital links. My hope is that, throughout these pages, you feel seen, heard, and understood by the Happy Teacher Revolution community.

The Green Rule

If there are suggestions that do not align with you and for you, don't use them! Follow the green rule: If it sounds like a green light for you then go go go! If your body, your heart, your spirit don't give you the green light, then toss the suggestion out. Not everything may land for you, and that's okay. The purpose of this book is interactive, and I hope are you able to adapt these suggestions in a way that aligns best for you. There are nuances within each strategy suggested in these pages, nuances that I wish I could dive so much deeper into. I am also committed to boundaries integrated within this very book, which cannot account for the depth of nuances of your own identity, your geographical location, and so many other factors.

Positive Relations with Others

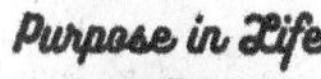

Follow the green rule as the sort of golden rule for your well-being as you engage with this resource and utilize suggestions within your own life. Green is the official color of mental health awareness, so symbolically the green rule is for you to prioritize your authentic knowing, self-awareness, and coming home to yourself as you prioritize your wellness as number one.

For immediate emotional support in the USA, call 988 to connect to a counselor.

HAPPY TEACHER REVOLUTION:
THE EDUCATOR'S ROADMAP TO CLAIMING & SUSTAINING JOY

PERMISSION SLIP FOR SELF-EXPLORATION IN WELL-BEING

Dear Reader,

You are not being volun-told to take care of yourself. Rather, you have the opportunity to claim and sustain your well-being as your own by exploring strategies related to prioritizing your well-being if they align for you. If you choose to accept this invitation to make a committment to your well-being, please confirm and consent via the form below.

Regards,
Danna Thomas
Author

**Please complete the lower section of this form, detach it, and hang it in your workspace as soon as possible.

I, (Name)____________________, give permission for myself to unapologetically prioritize my own well-being. I acknowledge the following details of the journey:

- I choose to be present
- I choose to be authentic to myself and my needs
- I choose to set boundaries
- I choose to claim joy as my own

____________________ ____________________

Signature Date

Happy Teacher Revolution:
The Educator's Roadmap to Claiming & Sustaining Joy

Figure 0.1 Permission Slip for Self-Exploration in Well-Being.

PART I

Investing in Yourself

Self-care is not self-serving. Self-care is OTHER focused. It's about having MORE and BETTER to give to the people and things you care about. There's a bit of a low anti–self-care grumbling in some parts of the teacher community. Some of this grumbling stems from the misidentification of self-care. Society at large defines self-care as a set of luxuries and indulgent habits which provide temporary satisfaction or relief. There's also a notion that self-care or, rather, the focus on one's own mental and emotional health means that students' needs will be somehow neglected. The reality is that the focus on "self" means increased capacity to serve and love others. We can no longer perpetuate the narrative that "good teachers" place themselves last. We have to understand the intersection of what's good for teachers and students. We have to believe that what's good for teachers is also good for students. This is your permission to let go of any guilt or shame you feel about prioritizing YOU. Your investment in self will pay dividends in the form of your IMPACT on your students and the people you care about.

—Alexis Shepard, former Middle School Educator, South Carolina

You truly are the one in the driver's seat when it comes to beginning the journey of your self-care. Making an investment in yourself is a transactional process that requires you to have some skin in the game. This investment may look like time, energy, space, and money spent on the best return on investment that possibly exists: *yourself.*

Your commitment to read this very text, this very research and collection of educators' perspectives, has taken some front-loading to begin to be present and to receive that information. Step 1 is to be open to these uploads of self-awareness. Step 2 is actually taking action to implement these practices. This text is a revolutionary pattern interrupt in shifting language to frame research-based conversations around educators being less stressed to educators increasing well-being.

Maslow's hierarchy of needs is actually something that I want to debunk in terms of one level being more important in the hierarchy or a foundational requirement in order to achieve the next. Rather, I argue that basic human survival needs and a sense of safety are just as important as cultivating a sense of belonging.

Furthermore, feeling competent is especially necessary in a profession that has room to be valued by society at large . . . especially a profession that requires such intense demands leading to a feeling like it's constantly Groundhog Day as new initiative after new initiative arrives. In my global listening campaign to collect anecdotal data to curate the research in this guidebook on educator well-being, I heard teachers share that they don't understand why despite having 20-plus years under their belt, the job continues to be getting harder and less manageable. Compared to other professions, the demands of educators have snowballed, intensified, and required them to keep wearing more and more hats.

The foundation of investing in yourself is knowing that you are worth investing in. Before we can foster connection with others and enact systemic change, the first step is to cultivate a sense of connection within oneself. This, in turn, is the most radical act of revolutionary change in terms of prioritizing your health and well-being and being an advocate for these tenets within a system that was not designed with your personal health and well-being in mind.

We cannot individualize our way into supporting systemic change around the well-being of adults working within any type of caregiver capacity within the education system. And yet the first step in every journey starts with the self. We cannot become a collective of individuals who align with supporting the mental health and well-being of educators until we perpetuate and deepen our own personal practices of self-care. Nothing I am about to share is a one-size-fits-all solution; rather it is an opportunity for you to personalize your learning plan for deepening your own understanding of about yourself.

As Róisín (2022) has said:

> The nature of self-care's commodification has meant that we've lost track of how personal this journey is. We all have our own traumas, fears, needs, and therefore our own specifications, idiosyncrasies. With such an overwhelming choice, it can be difficult to know what we need as individuals, how to *care for our own damn self*. . . . Caring for yourself means taking a giant leap toward yourself. You have to put yourself in your own driver's seat. (p. 164)

1

Tending to Your Basic Needs

So much of the narrative about what it means to be a teacher involves "doing without," or being a martyr. Pushing aside basic self-care—things like getting enough sleep, drinking enough water, actually using your sick days when you don't feel well, and using the bathroom when you need to use the bathroom—may seem noble, but think: Who benefits from your lack of basic self-care? Not you. And definitely not the kids, who are left to deal with a teacher who decided to teach through the flu, hold their bladder until the end of the day, or allow themselves only four hours of sleep on school nights. Your basic self-care is as essential to your teaching as professional development: Both you and your students suffer and pay the price when you don't get it. (Oh, and your loved ones, too. I can promise you that they aren't fans of when you neglect your basic self-care, either.)

In my discussions with teachers and administrators from across the country, I have met many veteran education professionals who have become so accustomed to putting others' needs first that they've neglected their own self-care to the point of making themselves chronically ill. I've also seen many new teachers working at unsustainable levels as they make the transition from being a student to being a teacher, pushing ahead even when they are exhausted. Now, as I write these words in late 2021, our nation is seeing what happens when educators who are already straining to do all that they can for others are also forced to work through a pandemic in, at best, questionable safety.

Simply applying more energy and more time to our jobs does not fix problems that are systemic in nature. Attempting to power through situations that are beyond our control puts us in danger and, ultimately, allows the systems that have put us into this position to continue to function. Trying to keep up with unsustainable demands leaves us exhausted, frustrated, and, often, questioning whether we should stay in the field. We're also doing a disservice to our students when we don't take care of our basic needs: Studies have shown that when high job demands and stress are combined with low social-emotional competence and classroom-management skills, poor teacher performance and attrition increase. Indeed, "understanding and uncovering negative emotions related to external stressors is the first step towards a better performance, a higher degree of professional satisfaction, and consequently, a higher level of teacher retention (Montgomery and Rupp, 2005, p. 483). In a study of New York City fourth- and fifth-grade students, higher teacher turnover had a significant negative effect on both math and language arts achievement; turnover was particularly harmful to lower-performing students (Ronfeldt, Loeb, and Wyckoff, 2013).

There's more to self-care than what we typically see on social media. Self-soothing practices like bubble baths can be fun and might help you clear your mind for a few minutes, but they don't address the issues that made you retreat to the tub in the first place. So, rather than list off a series of tips, this chapter will suggest ways in which you can be aware of your own basic needs and make changes to meet them in the moment. Think about it this way: Just as we might say to students who aren't demonstrating their fullest potential, "I care about you too much to not speak up. I care about you too much to deem this as acceptable behavior," we can say the same to ourselves regarding our own self-care and wellness. We can say: "I love this profession and my purpose too much to continue pouring from an empty cup because I know that is not sustainable in the long run." This is an opportunity to disconnect and detach from the martyrdom myth in order to show up as your fullest self tomorrow. Admittedly, this isn't always easy or comfortable: Schools are not designed for teachers' or administrators' well-being, and many of us carry the weight of trauma. No matter what you bring with you to work each day, know that you are not alone.

DISCOVER WHAT WORKS FOR YOU

I can hear a lot of secondary teachers saying "Oh my gosh, what is this?" when it comes to approaching well-being professional development that focuses on self-care.

—Rachel, former Social Studies Teacher and Supervisor, Maryland

The more I am learning and experiencing, the more I see that mindfulness is a practice that is good for me and my life right now. Other people might become more mindful and aware of who they are in different ways, so I don't think that it should be prescribed.

—Middle School Language Arts Teacher, Colorado

While this book can list a number of self-care options, you are the expert in *you*. Where do you notice that nurturing, "coming-home" type of experience, the one that feels like your bucket is being filled?

Instead of tuning into ourselves and our own individual experiences, oftentimes we're directed by someone else's ideas of what self-care *should* look like. In fact, recent studies show that the internet is the first stop when it comes to searching for self-care strategies (Rennis, McNamara, Seidel, and Shneyderman, 2014). But only *your* body can tell you what *you* need. Our bodies send us cues for us to listen to, but we have to be the ones not only to listen (before it gets too loud) but also to act on these cues in supportive ways that are just as unique as we are. This is especially important to note because not everyone has our best interests at heart: Self-care is now a $10 billion industry that continues to expand in the United States and around the world with the sole focus of commodifying self-care (Myers, 2014).

> *Define your own unique version of self-care.*

Choose practices and behaviors that help you to feel competent, creative, awake, and full of life. If it works, keep trying it. If it doesn't work, ditch it. There is no body of research to support a single, quick-fix solution. It's up to you to discover what works best for you.

PRACTICE SELF-CARE COMPETENCE

My self-care has been omission. Places, spaces, and people.

—Anleeta, Elementary School Special Educator, Chicago Public Schools, Illinois

VIDEO CLIP 1.1

Anleeta discusses how her experiences as an educator have shown how self-care is a culmination of one's physical and mental health.

https://www.wiley.com/go/happyteacherrevolution

Often, when we think of self-care, we think of things to add to our lives: mindfulness, yoga, a walk outside, time for ourselves. However, self-care can also mean removing harmful or negative influences from your life. It can mean ending relationships with individuals who don't support you and your best interests. It can mean not engaging in an argument with someone who is not committed to understanding you. It may mean removing yourself from abusive situations, people, friendships, or work environments. Delete the negative influences in your life to support your personal well-being and actively practice your own social-emotional competence in doing so. A teacher's own social-emotional competencies and well-being are key factors influencing student and classroom outcomes (Jennings and Greenberg, 2009). Sometimes saying "yes" to the committee, extra event, or additional activity outside of your job description is doing a disservice to your students if you are putting that commitment above your own social-emotional well-being.

Consider which elements are weighing on you.

Is there something holding you down that isn't necessary anymore? Maybe it's time to take it out of your backpack and let it go. Do you need to lead multiple committees? Do you need to have a Pinterest-perfect bulletin board that changes every week? Do you need to be available to parents or colleagues after 9:00 p.m.? Once you've established boundaries, people tend to respect them.

MAINTAIN YOUR SELF-CARE

Self-care is never one and done; it's continual.

—High School Teacher, New York

Running on the treadmill has its benefits, but consider the difference between a one-time run and ongoing cardio. Or consider how one session of therapy may be helpful, but what is truly worthwhile is the long-term investment in yourself. We live in a quick-fix world, but self-care isn't about "fixing" anything. Rather, it's an opportunity to nurture yourself as you already are. Consider it like maintenance for your car. If you own a car you have to make sure to regularly add gas, change the oil, check the brakes, and so on. Not just when there's an emergency, but as a continual practice.

According to research, more frequent participation in self-care activities relates to enhanced well-being (Richards, Campenni, and Muse-Burke, 2010), and previous research has found direct effects of self-care on self-awareness and well-being (Coster and Schwebel, 1997).

Self-care frequency data in a high-stress job like teaching is not easy to come by, but a recent study shows that US medical students who engage in self-care report less stress and a higher quality of life. Their findings suggest that US medical students who report high engagement in a wide array of self-care activities may experience some protection from the negative relationship between stress and quality of life (Ayala et al., 2018). For caregivers, self-care is essential.

> *Treat self-care like you treat your cell phone.*

Do you take care of recharging your phone more than you recharge your own self-care? How do you recharge? And are you doing it more or less often than you're recharging your digital devices? Don't wait until the last minute to recharge yourself, or until things start glitching or going haywire. Plug into self-care even when your battery is already 99% charged.

LISTEN TO YOUR BODY

I had repeated UTIs. . . My physician said to me, "It's a nurses and teacher profession disease: They don't take bathroom breaks."

—Elementary Teacher, New York

I remember lying in the hospital bed and I thought, "I'll finally get to rest."
—High School Biology Teacher, North Carolina

Many educators are empaths, tuned into the physical and social-emotional needs of others, often before themselves. While this level of attunement isn't something we should shame or eradicate, I propose that we also integrate a practice called body awareness, defined as "an attentional focus on and awareness of internal body sensations" (Mehling et al., 2009, introduction). Evidence suggests that an ability to recognize subtle body cues promotes overall health (Baas et al., 2004), yet our jobs often train us to ignore these cues.

Pay attention to the signals your body is sending you.

Signals from your body may be quiet or they may be loud. Listening to your body means eating well, going to the doctor when you need to, and actually using your personal and sick days. It also means getting enough sleep.

> Studies of teachers' response to high job strain reveal that they spend more time than most people ruminating about work-related issues and their brains take longer to unwind. Sleep hours suffer, as well as sleep quality. We need sleep to think clearly, react quickly, and create memories. It is during the later hours of sleep (especially between the sixth and eighth hour) when the brain releases the neurochemicals that stimulate the growth of the memory connections. (Willis, 2014)

The average teacher is reported to sleep six hours a night, falling short of the most valuable sleep time (Cropley, Dijk, and Stanley, 2006).

These might not sound like exciting solutions, but they work. By contrast, pushing yourself to work longer hours is not a badge of honor. You might think you'll gain valuable time from getting less sleep, but you won't be doing yourself or your students any good if your thinking, reaction time, and memory are impeded.

I CHOOSE TO
get outside and
GET MOVING
HAPPY TEACHER REVOLUTION

Figure 1.1

PRESENT YOUR AUTHENTIC SELF

I went into my first year of teaching with a weight. I was a victim of police brutality. . . . For a while, I dealt with a lot of anxiety [by] putting on a face for my students. . . . It felt like it took double energy to be present and be okay as their leader in the classroom.

—Elementary School Teacher, Louisiana

Teaching is a profession that often implies that we must be okay all the time, whether we're simply having a discouraging day or we're dealing with more serious issues. But our traumas and the invisible weights we carry in our body have an impact, not only on our health and well-being but also on our students' well-being and academic success. According to a longitudinal study, elementary school teachers who have greater stress and show more symptoms of depression create classroom environments that are less conducive to learning, which leads to poor academic performance among students. Students who began the school year with weaker math skills and had a teacher with more depressive symptoms had the lowest rate of achievement (McLean and Connor, 2015).

Don't assume that you can't bring your authentic self to your job. There is nothing wrong with answering a peer's "How are you?" with "Not so great today, but thanks for asking." Or with sharing with students that you've had a loss that has made you sad. Being authentic is an opportunity to bring your own humanity into the classroom. It takes far more energy to fake okay-ness than to be real. Additionally, pretending to be fine rarely results in authentic connections to your students or colleagues.

Be authentic.

SHOW UP FOR YOURSELF

There is no better feeling than when a child has that "Aha!" moment. However, in order to achieve that "Aha!" moment, teachers like myself often stay up late, neglect exercise, get into work early and survive on coffee that has turned cold. When you care for 20–30 bodies for eight hours a day, your mind starts to wonder how you can possibly care for one more person—even if it's yourself.

—Molly, Elementary Teacher and Teacher Coach of English for Students of Other Languages (ESOL), Maryland

VIDEO CLIP 1.2

Molly shares what keeps her going in the classroom—and the necessity of ensuring she has time for herself.

https://www.wiley.com/go/happyteacherrevolution

You can probably remember a time when you or a colleague kept food or even a change of clothes on hand for students, when you went to a school event to support a student, or when you followed up with family members when a student was in crisis. Consider how empowering it would feel to show up in an above-and-beyond capacity for yourself. Relentlessly. With the same passion and fervor that you show for others.

Research has shown that being kind to ourselves and practicing self-compassion improves our well-being. It also benefits the people around us. Researchers Kristin Neff and Andrew Costigan (2014) have argued that having a kind attitude toward ourselves actually makes us better able to look at our mistakes and make real changes.

Spend five minutes practicing active self-compassion.

As we practice staying in tune with ourselves and our basic needs, we become better able to ground ourselves in our own self-identity, understanding who we are and what we need without judging ourselves. Thus, we are better able to approach our students and loved ones from a place of nonjudgment and compassion. If you need to take five minutes to sit quietly before you join a faculty meeting, take it. Take a break from grading papers or sending emails to get something real to eat, not just a handful of snacks from the vending machine. Recognize those moments when you need to prioritize your own well-being and basic needs. Show up for yourself the way you show up for students.

I CHOOSE TO
schedule and
prioritize
WHAT REALLY
MATTERS
HAPPY TEACHER REVOLUTION

Figure 1.2

VIDEO CLIP 1.3

Morgan explains how a security breach put her and her students in danger and how she was left without support in the aftermath of the event.

https://www.wiley.com/go/happyteacherrevolution

CENTER YOUR WELL-BEING

The day a 25-year-old came into my classroom to try to fight one of my students or when a student stabbed my hand. . . . It would have been helpful to have time with a counselor to do deep breathing. But I had to keep teaching.

—Morgan, founder, The Greener Grass Project; former Middle School Educator, Maryland

[For] a lot of my friends who struggle with mental health, what is offered are more Band-Aid approaches. [They] do not feel supported in terms of the intensity of what is being offered. Also, there's an intensity of the emotions that we feel as teachers.

—High School Teacher of English as a Second Language (ESL), Tennessee

I want to advocate for my physical safety in terms of not getting COVID. I think a lot of it for me is that I don't know all of my rights so to speak. I think teacher training programs do a really poor job of making sure teachers know their rights. . . . What can I legally do or refuse to do in order to advocate for myself and my colleagues?

—Aubree, Fourth- to Fifth-Grade Teacher, Michigan

Often, organizations that put people in stressful situations (e.g., the military) have systems and infrastructure set up to support their personnel. Unfortunately, schools typically do not.

As of the writing of this book, COVID-19 and gun violence are some of the most publicized health threats in schools. However, there are also less-publicized health issues in schools: asbestos, lice, rodents, contagious diseases (schools rank among the "germiest" workplaces), trauma, and stress. Additionally, teachers are more likely to report being stressed at work than people in other professions, and tons of research suggests that stress can weaken the immune system (Will, 2020). Perhaps these factors are why teachers are more susceptible to certain types of infections than other workers (Kovess-Masféty, Sevilla-Dedieu, Rios-Seidel, Nerrière, and Chee, 2006).

> *An educator who feels unsafe, uncared for, and devalued cannot give their full selves to their work. Basic human needs extend to those who teach as much as they do to those who are to be taught.*
>
> — Christopher Emdin, Professor of Education, University of Southern California

Sometimes we may need to acknowledge that the education system we are working within was not designed with our well-being as caregivers in mind. Doing so starts your autonomy in acknowledging that you are your own first advocate. Consider the following suggestions when it comes to prioritizing your own well-being regarding personal sovereignty.

- *Learn where to go for help.*

  Know your rights and the support available to you so that you are ready when a serious issue strikes. Knowing the details of your contract, having specific contacts in Human Resources, knowing what your benefits plan offers (including leave time policies), and learning about Employee Assistance Programs will help you to advocate for your own health if you should need to. Know your union organization or a building representative that you are able to contact with concerns about safety.
- *Ask for help.*

  People who are in distress often reflexively respond that they are okay, even when they are not. Don't expect that others will be able to see past this common response if you need help. If your first attempt doesn't get the response you need, try someone else, moving up the chain of command in your building. Keep at it until you get your needs addressed. This might even mean speaking up beyond school—in the community, on social media, or even talking with media outlets if the situation warrants it. Your voice has power. When we reach out for help when we need it, we are doing the very same thing that we ask our students to do each day. We are practicing what we teach.

- *Leave if you have to.*

  As I write this portion of the book, COVID-19 is surging in the United States. After hearing more stories than I can count about teachers being required to teach in unsafe environments, there's one more suggestion I feel compelled to make here: Get out if you need to. This isn't a suggestion I make lightly; the strength of our schools relies on having skilled and experienced teachers and administrators, and each time one of us leaves the field, we are taking our hard-won experience with us. However, we cannot be the teachers or role models we want to be for students if we lose our health.

2

Cultivating Belonging

Self-care is a $10 billion industry that capitalizes on self-soothing and in some cases self-numbing. During some of my most unhappy times, I was spending every dollar of my disposable income investing in this "self-care" market. I put it in quotations because we know from Chapter 1 that we get to individually create a meaningful definition of self-care that is separate and different from the self-care capitalist industry. The fact that this search to achieve well-being is also through a very privileged lens is not to be discounted. Again, well-being is a capitalist profitable industry, and it has been marketed toward a very specific type of person through a lens of privilege. I am a single, white woman, and not only that but I wasn't investing in supporting a partner, a child or dependent, or aging family members. I was doing everything I thought that would lead me to pure happiness and bliss as defined by the self-care marketing machine: getting massages, facials, manicures, and pedicures, acupuncture, chiropractic care, retail therapy, real therapy, and on and on. And yet I would still be sitting in my car every morning in tears trying to collect myself before walking into the building each day. Cultivating a feeling of belonging is essential to our survival, and fostering that feeling of community is something that we'll explore in the next section and beyond.

We cannot individualize our way through collective well-being. That being said, this journey does begin with us and the authentic recognition that we are doing this self-work among one another within collective humanity. There must be a sense of belonging and community. We cannot go it alone.

No matter what age students we work with, one thing that is obvious is the craving for belonging. The feeling of sweaty palms gripping a lunch tray is visceral for me. And hearing stories of my students or their siblings feeling lonely, picked on, or like they don't fit in can bring about feelings from my own adolescence. When considering belonging, the antithesis could be termed rejection. Each of us has a core memory of the fear of rejection or rather a memory where we tried so hard to fit in or had to hide our most authentic selves in an attempt to feel like we belonged.

Sometimes I wonder how often individuals go into professional roles during adulthood working in schools to recreate or perhaps to create for the first time a sense of belonging. The depths of belonging are layered and multifaceted: belonging as a sense of belonging in this moment of time, belonging as a sense of belonging in this place, belonging as a sense of belonging in this physical body.

While Maslow put the need to belong midway up his hierarchy of needs, research over the past several decades suggests that belonging should be located closer to the base of the pyramid; it is as vital as food and shelter. Furthermore, this is true not just through childhood but *throughout* our lives (Cohen, 2022, p. 31).

Identify Belonging versus Fitting In

We can't cultivate belonging that's any greater than our sense of self-worth. So if you're struggling with belonging and feeling on the outside, the place to begin is self-work. True belonging, rather than pretzeling ourselves trying to fit in, is when we show up as our most authentic, vulnerable, imperfect selves. And research shows that cultivating authentic connection matters. The world's longest-lived people prioritize connection and have cultivated healthy lifestyles built on the foundation of belonging (Buettner and Skemp, 2016). Researchers further revealed across 148 studies performed on more than 300,000 participants that greater social connection is associated with a 50 percent reduced risk of premature death (Holt-Lunstad, Smith, and Layton, 2010).

Positive Relations with Others

Acknowledge your own sense of intuition when it comes to your sense of belonging.

> *I went through an experience a few years ago when I was the only Black teacher and was put down in so many ways and was not able to show what I was capable of, and I started feeling depression and didn't share that with anyone because I was afraid of the label of depression. Lack of self-care can lead to mental illness. The mean things that were said to me, I started to internalize it, and that's when the depression came. I had to go into the classroom with my students and put a smile on my face.*
>
> —Veteran Elementary Teacher, New York

> *Black kids really need Black teachers. I couldn't stay in a place where I didn't feel seen. I am the Black teacher that I wanted. Especially in this season as a Black educator I need to be filled up with Black people where I don't have to code-switch for a bunch of people. I just want to feel comfortable the way I feel. Teaching in a school with mostly Black and Brown students and Black and Brown parents.*
>
> —Tamara Russell, Elementary Educator, Florida

Ask yourself if you feel authentically seen in your current space . . . and if not, make a change to be in spaces where you don't feel compelled to code-switch. I'm not saying like belongs with like, and I'm also not saying to stay in a school or situation that is toxic and affecting mental health but rather to acknowledge your own intuition when it comes to feeling a sense of belonging in your community. We cannot operate in a vacuum, and community is important. If you are feeling isolated, make an intentional change to find an environment to be present in where you feel a sense of belonging.

Environmental Mastery

We are hardwired for belonging.

—Brené Brown, "Belonging + Self-Worth" (2023)

AIM FOR BELONGING

If teachers are not feeling a sense of well-being, the number one thing to focus on is fostering relationships. It's easier to do that. Not so easy for teachers to feel autonomous. Relationships are the biggest bang for your buck.

—Dr. Neesha Daulat, former Las Vegas Educator; current Assistant Professor, William James College, Massachusetts

VIDEO CLIP 2.1

In this video, Neesha describes the importance of belonging through her lens as a researcher in positive psychology studying the impact of teachers' emotional well-being.

https://www.wiley.com/go/happyteacherrevolution

When it comes to well-being, it's not enough to just be less burnt out; we need to aim for belonging. If we can reframe from a deficit mindset to instead have a more strengths-based approach, we can create opportunities to foster connectedness with others. I also have found that knowing that I'm not doing it alone has led to a presence of accountability and checking in with others who are prioritizing their personal growth as well.

Researchers suggest that lacking human connection carries a risk that is comparable to smoking up to 15 cigarettes a day. It is also well documented in scientific literature that the absence of human connection drives a person to the psychological brink of insanity (Holt-Lunstad et al., 2010). Greater sociability enhances brain health, and the lack of sociability threatens it (Cacioppo and Cacioppo, 2014).

> *Participate in activities and spaces outside of your classroom and professional identity.*

As someone who quarantined for weeks alone during the COVID-19 pandemic, I can attest to the effect of isolation on well-being. Instead of focusing on the negative, make a conscious choice to affirm or set a positive habit you hope to either continue or adopt from here on out. Now reach out to someone who you can share this goal with and invite them to also share a well-being goal or intention. Whether it's making an appointment related to your health, checking out a cultural exhibit or attending an event outside of your comfort zone or typical routine, or simply taking time to unplug and spending quality time with your loved ones or in nature, share this intention with someone else. Perhaps even participate in the intention with one another.

Positive Relations with Others

> *Have a space where people can get together and talk to each other. Get out of your classroom or space where you spend most of your day and instead get together in a space to talk to each other.*
>
> —Dr. Neesha Daulat, former Las Vegas Educator, current Assistant Professor, William James College, Massachusetts

Finding a sense of belonging within yourself by participating in activities or being present in moments where you feel like your most authentic self helps to deepen your perspective of who you "*be*" as a human *be*ing outside of your role as educator. Roy Baumeister and Mark Leary, two researchers of belonging, systemized a large body of work that highlighted that we have evolved as a fundamentally social species and have an instinct to seek social connection. According to Baumeister and Leary: "Human beings are fundamentally and pervasively motivated by a need to belong, that is, by a strong desire to form and maintain enduring interpersonal attachments" (1995, p. 522). We are hardwired to seek connection, so consider doing so with people and in spaces that help you feel a sense of belonging in the world beyond your identity in your professional role.

FULFILL YOUR AUTHENTIC SELF

Everyone operates on their own personal set of differentials because of the effort, energy, skills, and passions they are bringing to it. Do the things that work for you. Do the things that align to light your own fire of passion and purpose.

—Emma Barbato, former High School Special Educator, Owings Mills, Maryland

Stepping into your own authenticity not only increases a sense of belonging or at-homeness within yourself, but it also offers an opportunity to model to others what belonging truly looks like in action. When you are moving through the world operating as your most authentic self, you are able to cultivate a sense of belonging in the skin that you're in.

> Rather than outcasting the parts of ourselves which were once rejected, we work to reclaim those parts of ourselves that fear being seen, hurt, or left behind. We allow and include those parts of ourselves, moment by moment, strengthening our capacity for inclusion, for belonging. It is a practice of bringing the fullness of our presence to a moment, whether it's filled with rage or an upwelling of sadness, to say, "This too belongs." (Turner, 2021, p. 47)

Consider every day as graduation.

In learning to love and welcome the entirety of ourselves, we come into contact with a far vaster compassion for others. As Alice Walker shares in *The Temple of My Familiar*, "Helped are those who love others unsplit off from their faults; to them will be given clarity of vision" (1989, p. 393). Bring your authentic self to the spaces and places you're in.

There is a level of self-confidence that comes from operating in one's genius that surpasses whatever fleeting version one gets at a graduation ceremony.

Every day feels like graduation when one operates from a place of freedom and can always be one's authentic self.
—Christopher Emdin, Ratchetdemic: Reimagining Academic Success *(2021, p. 196)*

Ask yourself the following three questions at the beginning of each day: How can I be healthy? How can I be connected? How can I be purposeful?

Ask yourself if you are trying a certain way of "doing" rather than authentically "being." The best indication that you are trying to fit in rather than feeling a sense of belonging is how much pure exhaustion you feel during, leading up to, or following various encounters. There are folks I feel absolutely exhausted around; it is as if they are not quite able to hold full space for me or that I have to put on a front or a certain face during the interaction. When I am not living and being in my truth, I can feel it in my body. These encounters could be in person, online interactions, or just sensing within oneself something that simply does not align. Find the places and spaces where you can be your authentic self while acknowledging that we are in seasons of growth and deepening self-awareness.

Go to What You Know

"Go to what you know" as a strategy helps build relationships and improve a sense of belonging. Everything you already know about connecting with and establishing routines with students continues to be true. It's okay if this feels awkward. It's awesome even. Get curious and have fun with it. At the end of the day, you are the most important SEL content and curriculum.

—Chris Moore, Ed.S. Director of Mental Health & Social-Emotional Learning and School Psychologist, Salem-Keizer Public Schools, Salem, Oregon

Bring your personality into the community that you're in. At South by Southwest (where I spoke as a mentor), one teacher shared that they use nicknames in class or have student groups select their own group names to use throughout the year to create a sense of belonging within the classroom community. Create opportunities within the school day for self-care that look like both *you* and *your students* being your most authentic selves. Whether it's using nicknames, playing music you enjoy, or incorporating inside jokes into your day, bring your own uniqueness into the work that you do as a refreshing way to approach self-care.

> *Fitting in is about assessing a situation and becoming who you need to be to be accepted. Belonging, on the other hand, doesn't require us to change who we are; it requires us to be who we are.*
>
> —*Brené Brown,* The Gifts of Imperfection *(2010a, p. 25)*

Do the goofy thing.

In professional development, my sillier colleagues and I created a group name and table tent to display our group name that was based on a volatile penguin utilized in the early childhood curriculum with the tagline "I feel like I'm losing control." His name was Chilly and his well-being strategy was to utilize deep breathing to chill out. It made us laugh not only because of the double meaning of the familiar character but also because we could build belonging around the fact that there were times each of us really felt like we were losing control of the organized chaos that is the current reality of being an educator in the modern age. During a stressful time of the school year, we were able to be goofy with our team name, and it made the boring PD a little more bearable . . . and my former colleague and I still laugh about it to this day. We laughed while simultaneously remembering to simply take a breath during the moments that started to feel out of our control. Having a sense of humor helped make the day seem a little more bearable and also facilitated a sense of connection among the adults.

REACH OUT FOR SUPPORT

> *Therapy, reframing self-talk (not all your thoughts are true), self-compassion, letting go of perfection. Recently things got really hard, but talking to my health care provider helped SO SO MUCH and has been a huge part of making me feel like not only a functioning human but as a worthy teacher. I also try new things that don't have anything to do with teaching (cycling, yoga, strength training) and surround myself with people who build me up.*
>
> —Mariel Stein, former Early Childhood and Special Educator, New Jersey

If you've tried the suggestions already mentioned and are still feeling isolated, look for help with your emotional well-being. This would include both asking for encouragement and seeing professional mental health help. We cannot count on others to read our minds, and we also are invited to practice self-advocating and naming what we need. Also keep in mind that reaching out may feel cringey, awkward, and uncomfortable, but give yourself the opportunity to even be awkward together in community. Maybe awkwardness is where we all belong. We all have so much fear around groups, around sharing, around wanting to connect (Turner, 2021). When it comes to seeking help for yourself, know that shame breeds in silence. When you are able to reduce your isolation by making a connection with another person or health professional, you are not only helping your body but you are reprogramming the isolationist mindset and interrupting the pattern of feeling like you have to shoulder it alone.

> *I remind myself to remember that I don't always see myself clearly. When I get discouraged, I gather up my squad, express my insecurities, and ask for encouragement. They never fail to give it, and I never fail to gain new confidence in myself.*
>
> —Molly, ESOL Educator, Maryland

Ask for encouragement.

Another version of this tip is to post on social media and ask for encouragement; people *love* to give it. Remember, asking for help is a strength. Doing so takes vulnerability and courage—especially when the help you ask for relates to your sense of self-worth and overall mental health.

3

Feeling Competent

There's no way to ignore it: Education professionals are faced with the most direct demands of our society in the name of serving and supporting children. Our society has no safety nets, and the result is that teachers are expected to meet many of children's basic needs. When students come to school without academic background knowledge, when they live in food deserts, when they are living with trauma, school is child care, school is food, school is love, school is teaching us to be strong. School is doing all of these things that are not a part of academic education.

At the same time, teachers are finding themselves in the midst of polarizing issues, such as COVID-19 protocols and politicized arguments about what should and should not be taught in schools. That is not to mention perennial debates in education about things like the "right" way to teach reading or math.

No pressure, right?

In every profession, people worry about whether they're doing a good job. But in our field, where children's welfare is at stake and when forces outside our schools scrutinize our work according to their own agendas, our worries about how well we're doing our job can be overwhelming. Feeling competent can also pertain to everyday concerns—instruction, classroom management, and managing the workload of getting grading done. Fake it till you make it or pretending everything is fine when it actually isn't are not healthy models for educators to adhere to. Studies indicate that it is vital for people to feel authentically competent. Indeed:

> Several field and experimental studies have investigated the relationship between psychological competence, psychological well-being, and work-life balance. Consistently, psychological competence has been associated with greater psychological wellbeing and work-life balance. (Fotiadis, Abdulrahman, and Spyridou, 2019)

Research shows that higher levels of competence correlate positively to psychological well-being in addition to other psychological needs, such as hedonic happiness and life satisfaction (Cordeiro, Paixão, Lens, and Sheldon, 2016). When we feel incompetent at completing daily tasks and overcoming challenges, we become professionally inadequate (Maslach, Schaufeli, and Leiter, 2001). These feelings of inadequacy are a component of burnout (Daulat, 2020).

I'm struggling with feelings of esteem currently—not equating my self-worth to the classroom because, let's face it: We will never be made to feel that we are good enough. It's incredibly disheartening.

—Nicole, Pre-K Educator, Baltimore, Maryland

Our self-worth extends beyond our job. This chapter includes actionable strategies from real teachers who have struggled with real issues around feelings of self-competency—a component of self-acceptance.

MANAGE WITH MINDFULNESS

I kept feeling like I wasn't doing enough, but I also felt like I was completely maxed out.

—Martha, Elementary Educator, Maryland

Many of us, myself included, wear ourselves out to a point of exhaustion by burning the candle at both ends. When we spread ourselves so thin without tending to our mental health and well-being, we can feel overwhelmed and exhausted and want to just curl up into a ball. But mindfulness can help. Mindfulness can be defined as simply as being aware in the present moment.

In an age with constant demands, distraction, and seemingly never-ending to-do lists, it can sometimes feel impossible to just *be*. But the benefits of mindfulness are tangible. The American Psychological Association cites mindfulness as a strategy for alleviating anxiety, depression, and pain (Lu, 2015). But mindfulness doesn't just seem to boost mood and perception—the effects go deeper (Williams, 2017). Mindfulness practice can shrink the brain's jumpy fight-or-flight center, the amygdala (Taren et al., 2015).

While mindfulness can be a lifetime study, aided by classes, books, and instructors, it can also be something that you work on in manageable increments each day. Consider a moment that regularly occurs for you day to day. Whether it's brushing your teeth, making coffee, walking the dog, or listening to the first song on shuffle on your phone, do the task mindfully. Be in that moment and be present. Take in the sight, sounds, taste, feeling of that moment. Practice a mindful moment each day as a way of personal check-in to tune into yourself rather than the world around you. Mindfulness is about putting down all the balls that we have juggling to be completely focused on the present moment. Think monotasking instead of multitasking.

> *Prioritize mindfulness.*

ACCEPT SOME DISCOMFORT

> *I was losing so much of my personality trying to recover from the day. I was miserable. And when I went home I didn't feel like talking to friends, I didn't feel like making dinner. After everything else, coming home and thinking about cooking felt impossible.*
>
> —Claire Jackson Stumbras, Chief Program Officer, Teach for America Twin Cities; former Middle School Educator, Maryland; former School Leader, Minnesota

> *Sit in it. Feel it. That moment of OOF hits. Sit there. Don't be so quick to jump out.*
>
> —Former Elementary Educator, current Adjunct Professor, Florida

Figure 3.1

VIDEO 3.1

Claire reflects on her experiences as a new teacher, recalling how her wellness was not a priority, and how that impacted her students. She explains that she has recentered her priorities and acknowledges that the systems educators currently work within rarely support their wellness.

https://www.wiley.com/go/happyteacherrevolution

Trying to avoid discomfort can lead us to impulsive self-numbing (distracting ourselves with our phones) or self-soothing (a Netflix binge or another glass of wine) rather than addressing what is causing the discomfort. These actions don't resolve the issue and set us up for having to face the same issue the next day. When we acknowledge our discomfort, we can identify what's causing us pain, and we can take intentional action that turns our discomfort into an opportunity for growth.

Acknowledge discomfort.

Acknowledging discomfort means admitting that we might be uncomfortable—lonely, uncertain, stressed, even scared. The practice of acknowledging discomfort activates the region of the brain that controls planning, which helps us to avoid impulsive, unhelpful reactions. Sitting with our discomfort also helps us to recognize that the discomfort is temporary (Brancatisano, 2016).

AFFIRM YOURSELF

> *I swear I could write a book on my journey through burnout. For me, I had to come to the realization that I couldn't let my career define my identity. I am so much more than a teacher.*
>
> —First-Grade Teacher, Missouri

Self-affirmations are powerful. In a study, researcher Christopher N. Cascio and colleagues (2016) used functional magnetic resonance imaging (fMRI) to find that self-affirmation increases activity in the reward centers in the brain. These areas—the ventral striatum and ventromedial prefrontal cortex—are the same reward centers that respond to other pleasurable experiences, such as eating your favorite food or winning a prize.

Bank yourself a pep talk.

When you are feeling affirmed, take a moment to create a video or take a photo to capture the moment. Don't be critical of it; it's something that is just for you. When you have forgotten how awesome you are, review the video or photo to remind yourself. Start an album on your phone of these digital artifacts to scroll through when you need an uplifting reminder. Or take a moment to write down an affirmation at the beginning or end of your day. Then read it aloud. Here are some affirmation examples:

- "I am capable."
- "I am planting new seeds with intention and purpose."
- "I am worthy of my dreams."
- "I am constantly growing, evolving, and becoming my best self."

CREATE ROUTINE

I wake up an hour earlier and listen to jazz like Miles Davis and Coltrane. I start my day drinking lemon water or coffee, and do a bit of reading, maybe 10 to 15 minutes. During the day I try to take moments where I can close my eyes and think about my intentions for the remainder of the day and give myself a moment to take in the space and think of things I'm grateful for.

—Tre'Shawn, Early Childhood Educator, Nevada

I work early instead of working late, so that gives me an hour to get my brain in a spot to get it where I need it to be. That is how I've created a routine in my life to support my esteem.

—Dana, Fourth-Grade Science Teacher, New Jersey

The benefits of routine are far-reaching. Building a routine helps self-care practices become a habit. Studies have found that routine was linked to improvements in mood and cognitive function and to a notable decrease in developing major depression (Lyall et al., 2018). According to cognitive behavioral therapy clinical psychologist Dr. Steve Orma, routine helps with stress management: "To manage anxiety, you need to consistently check in with yourself about what you're worrying about, then address it" (quoted in Robins, 2017).

Consider your day-to-day life.

Is there an opportunity to build a routine that aligns to your wellness goals and values? Where can you offer yourself an opportunity to create a regular practice of a specific routine that can ultimately become a habit? Can you pair that routine with mindfulness or with a self-check-in to actively acknowledge any discomfort that may be showing up for you during your routine? If we couple a new routine with an already existing one, often there is an increased likelihood of a new practice actually sticking. For example, I wanted to start journaling in the morning so I attached that new routine with an already existing one, which is brushing my teeth.

Stay Focused on You

The Pinterest-perfect teachers make me want to leave the field. All you see is that perfection. No one sees the home life or personal life component.

—Liz, Pre-K and K Special Educator, Maryland

Video 3.2

In the video, Liz explains how letting go of comparing herself to other educators has helped her to be a stronger educator.

https://www.wiley.com/go/happyteacherrevolution

We are pinned against each other instead of lifting each other up. It's a competition now because of how test-driven and data-driven the school culture is. There's so much that's out of your control.

—Amanda, ESOL Educator, Maryland

In a world where the visibility to the outside that others offer is so often curated, we can find authentic esteem in focusing internally and in affirming

ourselves intrinsically. The term "self-concept clarity" refers to the extent to which someone truly knows who they are and their own sense of themselves. Research has found that self-concept clarity mediates the relationship between stress and well-being (Ritchie, Sedikides, Wildschut, Arndt, and Gidron, 2011). Also, having a clear and stable view of ourselves can help us in our relationships (Lewandowski, Nardon, and Raines, 2010).

Drop Something

My friend is one of the best teachers I've ever seen. If she says, "Nope, I can't handle that right now," she does it in a way that is not mean or rude. She makes it understood that for her personal good she is unable to do the extra job.

—Kindergarten Teacher, New Mexico

Often, productivity is valued over purpose, busyness is considered an accolade, and the scarcity mindset feels like truth. Prioritizing self-care feels like another task on our never-ending to-do lists. In fact, the ultimate version of self-care is doing *less* instead of taking on *more*. This is true for both teachers and administrators alike.

Overextending ourselves puts us on a path out of the classroom. Overall teacher attrition rates in the United States are around 8 percent, over twice the rate of countries such as Finland, Canada, and Singapore (Darling-Hammond, Furger, Shields, and Sutcher, 2016). New teachers leave at even greater rates—"somewhere between 17 percent and 30 percent over their first five years of teaching" (ibid., p. 15). Anecdotal evidence suggests that teacher and administrator attrition is even higher in the wake of COVID-19, and more teachers are retiring earlier than ever before. "In 2022, more than half (55%) of [National Education Association] members say they are more likely to leave or retire from education sooner than planned because of the pandemic, almost double the number saying the same in July 2020" (National Education Association Policy Statements, 2022).

It's okay to say no. Or at least say "I need time to think about it."

Consider the demands in your life at this moment of time. Are there opportunities that you said "yes" or "maybe" to doing that now feel draining?

Consider removing them—or at least temporarily suspending them. If setting something down feels difficult (or impossible), consider how much more effective you can be in your other roles without this drain. When you've decided what to say no to, approach the conversations from a place of love—for both yourself and your community. It's okay to say no. It's okay to change your mind. It's okay to advocate for your needs. Consider your sustainability not only in this profession as a teacher or leader but as a human being.

FACE PROCRASTINATION

My way to handle stress is avoidance. I avoid everything. I don't like confrontation, I don't like conflicts, so I avoid it. And that's self-sabotaging behavior.

—Aubree, Third-Grade Teacher, Michigan

Trying to start a task seems exhausting so I procrastinate. Then I end up working late; sometimes pulling an all-nighter to make a deadline. Which exhausts me. It's a horrible merry-go-round I want to get off.

—Anonymous, Fourth-Grade Math/Science Teacher, Texas

Procrastination and lack of self-confidence often go hand in hand. It's important to name that procrastination is real, and often it feels like it is beyond our control. Procrastination has more to do with emotions than it does with time, according to researchers (Flett, Haghbin, and Pychyl, 2016). Recent research reveals that the amygdala—a brain structure that processes emotions and controls motivation—is larger in procrastinators. These individuals also had poorer connections between the amygdala and the dorsal anterior cingulate cortex, the part of the brain that helps keep us on track by blocking out competing emotions and distractions (Pathan, 2018).

Create an accountability time lapse.

To keep herself accountable, educator and influencer Valencia Clay records time-lapse videos of herself while she's grading papers, planning, setting up her classroom, and doing coursework for her graduate classes. She models what the process looks like not only as her own productivity hack but also to build a community of accountability in her method of "g.r.o.w"—which stands for "grow beyond creative barriers." This methodology is also discussed in a guidebook titled

Grow Beyond Creative Barriers G.R.O.W. Productivity Guide: 100 Self-Paced Strategies (Clay-Bell, 2023).

Chunk the big stuff; cluster the little stuff.

Most commonly, procrastination shows up for educators in regard to grading and paperwork deadlines. Is there an opportunity to backward-plan the time it takes to grade utilizing small chunks rather than pulling an all-nighter at the end of grading season? How can you break down a larger task on your to-do list into smaller chunks that feel more tolerable?

Find a quick win.

Whether it's the bulletin board, sending an email, or scheduling the teeth cleaning you've been putting off, take a moment to relish a small win to cross off of your list. Your quick win can also be one of the small tasks that chips away at a larger item on your to-do list. Remember what Desmond Tutu once said: "There is only one way to eat an elephant: a bite at a time."

Try mindfulness meditation.

As procrastination researchers from Carleton University in Ottawa, Canada, explain, meditation reshapes our brains: "Research has . . . shown that mindfulness meditation is related to amygdala shrinkage, expansion of the pre-frontal cortex, and a weakening of the connection between these two areas" (quoted in Study International Staff, 2018). When we're able to gently and deliberately bring our attention back to the breath in meditation, we're developing the skill to do the same with the tasks we face. Doing so enables us to move from focusing on emotions to focusing on action.

According to Patricia Jennings (2015b), mindfulness helps teachers . . .

- Understand our own emotions better.
- Communicate more effectively with students.
- Manage students we find difficult.
- Set up a positive learning environment.
- Strengthen our relationship with students.
- Slow down when we need to.
- Build community.

STRENGTHEN YOUR KNOWLEDGE

In the midst of COVID, we had to record YouTube videos. I'm pretty tech savvy, but I still struggled. You have to be vulnerable enough to ask for help. Or admit you don't know.

All professional development (PD) does not come from another teacher or sitting in PD. You have to be the one that is seeking out the information because it's not just going to find you. If someone tells you to check out this website or recommends a resource, don't just check it out. Actually dive into the website. You may have to read more than one article.

—Erika, Elementary Educator, Maryland

VIDEO 3.3

In the video, Erika from Baltimore shares some helpful hints when it comes to prioritizing your well-being and setting helpful boundaries.

https://www.wiley.com/go/happyteacherrevolution

When you don't feel competent, ask for help or look for resources that can help you to grow professionally. If you don't speak up, you are at risk of intensifying feelings of shame as you continue to suffer in silence. Shame creeps in when we doubt our competence, and it eats away at our competence as it grows. Brené Brown has spent decades researching the human condition, particularly shame and empathy. Her advice for when we feel shame?

Ask for help and lean into humility.

> Practice courage and reach out! We need courage, compassion, and connection. ASAP. Shame hates it when we reach out and tell our story. It hates having words wrapped around it—it can't survive being shared. Shame loves secrecy. The most dangerous thing to do after a shaming experience is hide or bury our story. When we bury our story, the shame metastasizes. (2010a, p. 10)

When you get good guidance or advice, put it to use. Rather than trying to be all-knowing with your students or colleagues, be a person. Be humble.

When you talk to your students to build connections and relationships with them, teaching becomes so much easier. Students learn when you model social-emotional learning skills yourself. Colleagues also learn what adult social-emotional learning looks like in action by bearing witness to you modeling these practices.

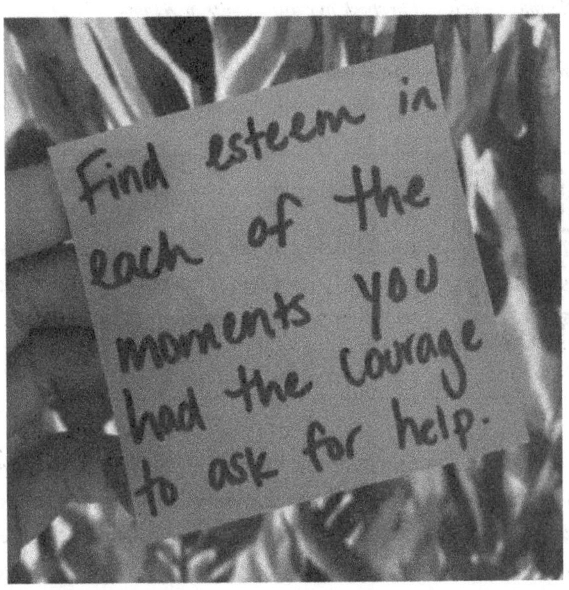

Figure 3.2

4

Reaching Beyond Everyday Life

Once you
Accept
That you are
Valuable,
Your life
Will change.

—Lyn Patterson, Reprinted with Permission.

We are so much larger than our past experiences, the chaos of the world, or the current season of emotions. As we open up to receive more joy, belonging, and self-acceptance, being open to the depth of the full spectrum of human emotion can be extremely uncomfortable.

Consider the metaphor of driving a car toward an ultimate destination. The road is the journey, the destination is your goal, and the driver is your highest, most aware sense of self. And yes, there are passengers joining you for the ride. Think of Alanis Morissette's music video for her song *Ironic*, with all her "versions" of self: Instead, each of these passengers is something that may be uncomfortable . . . shame, grief, sadness, and the like. You don't toss those passengers out of the car; rather, you assert yourself as the driver continuing toward your destination while acknowledging that others are there for the ride. Reaching beyond yourself toward happiness also includes reaching inside yourself to shine light and shower love toward some of those curmudgeons in the car with you. All parts of yourself are welcome here.

Being a teacher feels more than a title on a résumé. In this day and age, when metrics track one's level of "influence" across social media and numerous other platforms, I argue that "teacher" fits the original and historical definition of "influencer." And considering the amount of influence teachers carry, take a moment to reflect on the level of larger influences that play a part in your own life.

Teaching feels like more than a job title not only due to the amount of influence you have, but also because teaching feels like part of one's identity. For this reason, teachers are a particular target market within the capitalist framework and also are very easy to identify from a marketing standpoint. People even include the fact that they are teachers on personal Instagram and social media accounts, in the short description of who they are and how they introduce themselves to the world. In many teachers' bios on social media, they include their role as teacher along with their name, pronouns, spirituality, and/or relationship status.

While this strong association to your career can be considered noble, heartfelt, and sincere, there's so much more to who you are beyond a job description. Often teachers will tell each other, in the spirit of self-care, that if you dropped dead today, your employer would have your replacement hired by tomorrow morning without a second thought. Given the teacher shortage, I'm not sure how quick the turnaround might be; nevertheless, it's important to consider what makes you who you truly are outside of the occupation you list on your résumé.

Reaching beyond the mundane or, rather, reaching *within* the mundane is where the contentment lies. It's noticing the gratitude, bliss, and connectedness with the trees outside the window, the neighbor from across the street, the stranger at the grocery store.

It's also okay to acknowledge that you may not quite know what contentment is yet. These practices of self-reflection, consideration of our interconnectedness with one another, and the greater call to action to make systemic change will help you clarify your unique personal goals and vision for who you are and who you get to be. At least such self-reflection will point you toward taking the next step.

Something deep inside drew me into the role of teacher and "Miss Thomas," and yet when I was teaching at Holabird Elementary/Middle School in Southeast Baltimore, there was just as strong a pull on my heart to serve an even larger purpose. It was a both/and moment, an opportunity to recognize the duality of both holding my current role and the immense importance of serving and supporting a group of learners . . . AND it was also recognizing that there would be a greater calling. I didn't realize it at the time, but that calling was to be a global advocate for the mental health and well-being of teachers. It was a greater call to action around naming the invisibility and insidious effects of trauma, systemic injustices, and complete neglect of caregivers as people. My call to action was bringing more humanity into this profession, specifically the big humans caring for the little humans.

You are the sky. Everything else—it's just the weather.

—Pema Chödrön

DANCE. SING. CREATE.

If we're not supposed to dance,
Why all this music?

—Gregory Orr, Poet and former Professor, University of Virginia
(and Educator who truly saved my life)

I took Gregory Orr's poetry seminar in college. I can absolutely testify that the arts saved my life and that his book, *Poetry as Survival,* helped. These strategies to dance, sing, write, or play are invitations to connect with your own creativity. Create, make, build, express for your own sake and not for anyone else. This is an opportunity for you to express and to do so uncensored; it is not necessary to share on social media or for anyone else to bear witness to.

My favorite form of creating is playing my saxophone. I started playing the sax in the fourth grade because of my hero, Lisa Simpson, and I've enjoyed rocking the blues ever since. When I suffered from anxiety and depression in high school, music as a form of expression and my relationship with my music teachers helped me not only feel like I could be my most authentic expressive self, but also that it was okay to *not* be okay. My teachers were my heroes who saved my life. I like to think of them as my emotional first responders who recognized subtle changes in my behavior and encouraged me to seek treatment and get help. Today, I am proud to say I chose life. I also still choose to pick up my saxophone to offer myself that creative outlet for my own well-being.

In Elena Aguilar's book *Onward* (2018), she suggests that creativity, imagination, and innovation are the missing ingredients in many school reform efforts. As Aguilar says, "School transformation almost always relies on deeply creative thinking" (p. 259). Being creative not only supports you in self-actualization; it also supports the actualization of systemic change.

I didn't realize that my experiences as a jazz improvisation musician would be so similar to my experiences as a teacher. It doesn't mean that I wasn't prepared, it means that I ended up developing a framework and skill set to draw on when life didn't go as planned. It was an invitation to be inventive. Educators possess the unspoken skills of being able to improvise, which is a dynamic aspect of creativity in and of itself. Consider where you can tap into the right hemisphere of the brain through the arts, whether it is improvising on a canvas, on an instrument, through dance, or another means that aligns with you.

Prioritize creativity accountability.

If you don't know where to start in holding yourself accountable to creativity, do something with your hands. Plant flowers. Bake bread. Doodle in a notebook or digitally create using Microsoft Paint (throwback!).

The next prompts invite you to create the space to explore your artistic expression. Some prompts refer to poetry, but feel free to act out, paint, play, or use any other form of creative expression. Or create your own prompts. Or disregard prompts altogether and give yourself the opportunity to improvise. There is no wrong way of creating; the only way to fail is by not allowing the creativity to be present. Consider these prompts as invitations, and check out the poems provided in Part II of this book.

- Write a poem from the perspective of yourself at the age of the students you teach.
- Write a poem from the perspective of one of your current or former students.
- Write a poem connecting a message in life that you live by with an academic concept you teach in your class.

PUT THINGS DOWN

I choose to disconnect and detach with love.
I choose the battles worth fighting.
I choose to let go.

—Happy Teacher Revolution, www.happyteacherrevolution.com

As I was writing this book, I realized that one of my personal coping strategies is attempting to have a semblance of control over the uncontrollable by showing up and stepping up for others. At times I've referred to this as an overdeveloped sense of responsibility. I realized that carrying things for others, whether it was a work task or another emotional load, also had a way of serving me by being a distraction and form of procrastination. I realized that it felt more comfortable, familiar, and practiced to prioritize others' needs over my own.

Today I acknowledge that there are responsibilities that are simply not mine to hold. There are things that I can put down even if it's temporary. And, in doing so, I acknowledge that I am creating a whole way of being, doing, and creating in the world. This pattern interrupt of creating from a place of nourishment rather than chaos is a whole new way of operating. It also is not an opportunity to shun the superhero part of myself but rather to determine how can I be a superhero for my inner child/

younger version of myself. How can I check in with my general sense of self and ask "Hey there, how are you *really*?" Recognize and give yourself permission to put things down sometimes. Also feel self-compassion in knowing you can pick things back up again later if doing so still aligns for you.

Write and say aloud affirmations that align with your truth.

I forgive myself for____.

I'm proud of myself for____.

I choose to give myself permission to____.

Consider using these affirmations to close out your workday or as part of an evening ritual. Perhaps even share these affirmations with your students as an invitation to be vulnerable, authentic, and purposeful around their own personal growth.

PLAN REST

You don't have to be superhuman to be a good teacher.

—Liz, Special Education Teacher, Maryland

"The point of doing nothing, as I define it, isn't to return to work refreshed and ready to be more productive, but rather to question what we currently perceive as productive."

—Jenny Odell, *How to Do Nothing: Resisting the Attention Economy* (2021, p.xii)

Consider planning your rest or intentionally doing nothing. The "one more thing" syndrome to go the extra mile or just heap one more thing onto the already overwhelming weight of responsibilities is something that feels so familiar to teachers. Schedule a day to see the sunrise and sunset. Or perhaps spend time around trees, a body of water, a public garden, or bear witness to the mountains. Wherever or whenever you are, take a moment to be present to the world around you and within you. The purpose of this rest is not to recuperate or be a better worker. The purpose of planning rest is for rest's sake in and of itself.

Figure 4.1

Schedule not scheduling.

Carve out intentional time to not *do* anything. Or at least schedule time to witness Mother Nature if the invitation to do nothing feels overwhelming or not right for you. Recognize that our biological systems are not designed or equipped to manage the constant barrage of alerts, demands, and nervous system elevation. One of my favorite resources around cultivating intentional stillness is *How to Do Nothing: Resisting the Attention Economy* by Jenny Odell of Stanford University.

Be gentle with yourself.

As you "self-actualize," be gentle with yourself in breaking these generational and systemic patterns. Know that *resistance* is a sign of work working! Plant a seed of well-being by incorporating these new habits and viewing them through a lens of gentleness. Know that your seed of intention will grow and in the future you will get to harvest your bounty in anticipation of future growing seasons.

SCHEDULE DATES WITH YOURSELF

Know that you are earning but most importantly deserving of taking space. The body has to believe that we can take space first. We spend so much of our time leading a schedule and serving others, so schedule a date night with yourself. When you take space for you and are deserving of love, we get to start having the self-actualization of who we BE without being in relation to someone else. We deserve it because we are human and it is part of the human experience.

—Taylor Gonzalez, former Baltimore City Educator; current Trauma Informed Embodiment Coach, Florida

VIDEO 4.1

In this video, Taylor walks through suggestions for self-actualization and opportunities for embodiment.

https://www.wiley.com/go/happyteacherrevolution

Taking time to be present with yourself is a radical act. Specifically, you have an opportunity to bring yourself pleasure, whatever that looks like in the moment. In her book *Belonging* (2021), Toko-pa Turner describes "embodied living" or being present in awareness in our own bodies, as involving "ourselves not only with goodness, but with the ache of longing and absence, including them in our way of going" (p. 145). In these "dates" with yourself or appointments to be with yourself, ask yourself:

> Can I be with my longing? Can I allow the emptiness of what is missing from me remain without trying to fill it with stand-ins and facsimiles? Can I be longing without expectation that it be soothed? Can I, in living with absence, become the presence it is so hungry for? (ibid.)

This habit will only add to your personal connections and your professional life. The ripple effect continues outward, but the most important point is that you are at the epicenter as the source of supporting yourself first and foremost.

Write yourself a love letter.

Take out the fancy pen and paper, draft a note on your phone with your favorite emojis, or maybe pull out an old journal to write a love letter to yourself. Create a playlist of love songs for yourself. Often iconic chart-topping hits refer to romantic love, but consider reframing those same love songs by looking in the mirror and serenading yourself.

Be present in your body.

Be present in your body. Give it exactly what it is asking for in this moment (or one of those things)—something that will make you feel good, that will bring pleasure to your physical body.

Take a moment, when you are within a community, whether it is virtual or in person, to drop into your body. I like to excuse myself to go to the restroom. After giving myself that solitude and alone time, I take a moment to close my eyes and take a couple deep breaths. I put a hand on my heart and drop into my physical body to collect observations as if they are scientific data.

The curiosity rather than judgment around these noticings is key. Observe if there is tension, stuckness, or tenderness in your body. Where does it live? How can you take a couple of deep breaths into the body? Similarly, drop into any physical experiences of pleasure in the body. Is there any part that feels particularly relaxed or easeful? Notice it. Not only does this practice cultivate an experience of belonging within the body, but it also gives you an opportunity to create space to be in the body in a group setting. You take the time to be with yourself and notice if your body is sending you signals in regard to how you feel within a particular community.

5

Engaging in Self-Care with Students

1

Start a Win Journal

Video 5.1

In this video, Fareeha, a Special Education Teacher in Baltimore, MD, describes utilizing a personal practice that has translated into her classroom.

https://www.wiley.com/go/happyteacherrevolution

In "The Power of Small Wins," Teresa M. Amabile and Steven J. Kramer write:

> When we think about progress, we often imagine how good it feels to achieve a long-term goal or experience a major breakthrough. These big wins are great—but they are relatively rare. The good news is that even small wins can boost inner work life tremendously. Many of the progress events our research participants reported represented only minor steps forward. Yet they often evoked outsize positive reactions. (2011)

In the video, Fareeha shares how she keeps a "win journal" to document her small wins at the end of each day. One reason this practice is so powerful is that a win journal is always there to remind you of your awesomeness—even during the tough days. A win could be as subtle as a student quietly showing trust in you or as obvious as being publicly thanked for your work. Reminding yourself of your wins after a long day can help you remember and ground yourself in your *why*. As a Student Services Coordinator in Putnam County, Tennessee, says, "There are days that are crazy stressful and there are nights that I go home and wonder 'Did I help anybody?' and I realize and reassure myself, yes, I did."

Not only did Fareeha create a win journal for herself; she also realized the benefit of sharing this strategy with her students. She "honors and celebrates each of the unique accomplishments in their own lives" by carving out time within the classroom not only to recognize the wins of individual students but also to honor collective wins of the class. This is exactly what strategies based on social-emotional learning look like in action within a classroom community.

Exercise Your Best Self

In her higher education psychology course, Christina Costa at Wayne State University shares a practice she holds with her college students called the best-self exercise. In the Best Possible Self exercise, developed by the University of Missouri's Laura King and Harvard's Jeffrey Huffman, you take 15 minutes to write about an ideal future life (1–10 years from now). Imagine everything is going as well as possible, from family and personal life

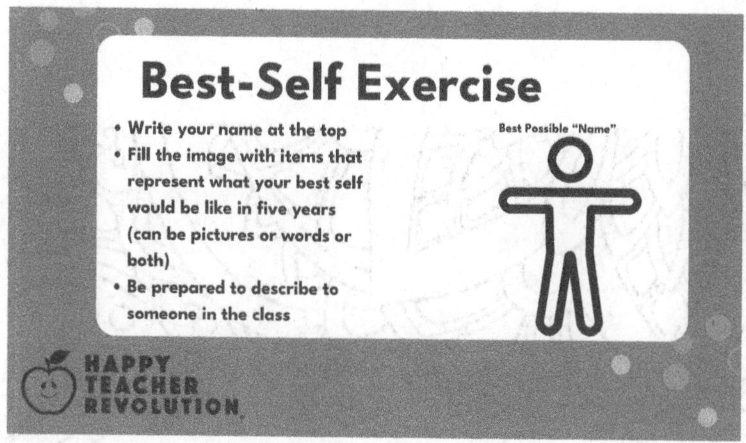

Figure 5.1 Best-Self Exercise.
Adapted from Christina Costa (2021).

to career and health. Be creative and specific and focus on your potential rather than any past shortcomings. Doing this daily for two weeks has been shown to increase positive emotion, possibly because it helps us identify goals, feel more in control of our lives, and maybe even decide to change things. When you identify a goal, you can take another day to journal about the steps you have taken to achieve it, imagining you are already there.

Practice Mindfulness Together

The benefits of mindfulness are numerous and were described in Chapter 3. Mindfulness has been found to positively affect well-being (Brown and Ryan, 2003). One of the best ways to integrate meditation in a classroom can be a short moment to hold space at the top of the class as "a moment to arrive." This intentional dropping into the present can last anywhere from 30 seconds to over a minute. It can also simply be a collective couple of deep breaths that you take together as a classroom community. You may even offer guidance on the collective breaths by cueing students to inhale through the nose and exhale from the mouth.

Breathwork is essential to feed our organs and systems. You can't preach self-care if you don't practice It. Model how to breathe in the anxiety then

Figure 5.2

expel it. Give kids the chance to be intentional, and give opportunities to model how to take care of themselves. If we don't support the adults who haven't moved through their own work on emotional intelligence, we aren't supporting the students in those spaces, either. Consider mindfulness about what you're consuming: hearing; scrolling; watching passively or actively. Consider silence, stillness, noninput, and sharing those opportunities with your students.

Mindful eating and mindful listening are also ways to integrate mindfulness in the classroom environment. Consider pairing up students and engage social-emotional learning strategies to encourage students to practice mindful listening. Not talking for an entire minute can be challenging, but providing space to feel seen and heard with a partner is an opportunity to foster both social-emotional learning and mindfulness in the classroom environment.

Environmental Mastery

6

Establishing Boundaries 1

Create Containers

I use communication methods that allow me the control to shut off communication. Or I won't put apps on my phone; that way I have to use a computer in order to check it instead. I deal with feelings of guilt so if somebody messages me and I see it, I feel like I have to answer it. Not even seeing it on my phone is what I do to protect myself from that.

—Heather, Elementary Educator, Maryland

Video 6.1

In this video, Heather explains some examples of boundaries that have helped her support her own well-being as an educator for Baltimore City Public Schools.

https://www.wiley.com/go/happyteacherrevolution

Set a container, a limit for when you are not available. For me, this was a 6 p.m. deadline on weekdays; I would no longer respond to work items until 9 a.m. the following business day. I didn't respond to work emails, calls, or texts from Friday evening until Monday morning. At first, this was incredibly frustrating to those who were accustomed to "Danna on demand." This boundary took some getting used to. But people, especially students' parents, learned that this was my expectation, and they began to adhere to this specific container and the boundaries I set for being able to reach me. Setting boundaries feels easier in a new place or at the beginning of a new year, but you can set them at any point. You may need to repeat your boundaries and remind others of them. Practicing new boundaries for both yourself and those around you may feel unfamiliar and clunky at first, but that is a sign of the work "working."

CULTIVATE SPACIOUSNESS

Set boundaries for yourself to give yourself space. Cultivate spaciousness and a practice of "wait and see" to check in with your body. Your body may send you signals to rest, to eat something, to go outside to breathe fresh air, to engage in movement, to sit in stillness, or something entirely different. In birthing this book and in the months before the manuscript was due, I had to set some firm boundaries with myself in my personal life. I made the commitment to have set plans only with family and for big travel plans I had already made. I would not commit to other in-person social plans at this time. Most people were kind and compassionate toward this boundary, but some questioned it. I got curious and noticed what came up when there was resistance to this boundary. I realized that the disappointment of others in me having this boundary was not my disappointment to hold. I also realized that when I set boundaries for myself to deliberately not fill up my schedule by automatically saying "yes" as a default response, I could be intentional about when, how, and even *if* I choose to react. It is empowering to say "no" or "not right now" or "I need to wait and see" rather than automatically agreeing. This intention to create space in my life is something I share because while it was not received warmly by all, I realized I needed to do it to champion my own needs and priorities.

PART II

Reflecting/ Integrating 1

RESILIENCE STRATEGIES FOR EDUCATORS
TECHNIQUES FOR SELF-CARE AND PEER SUPPORT

BUILDING A SELF-CARE ACTION PLAN

Vicarious (secondary) trauma, compassion fatigue, and burnout can be prevented. Doing so, however, requires a conscious effort to practice individual self-care strategies on a regular basis, both personally and professionally, to assist in managing vicarious stress.

Here is one example of how to build a self-care plan. There are six categories. These include:

1. Physical Self-Care:
The things I do to take care of my body in healthy ways. Examples include: sleep; nutrition; exercise; and, regular health care visits. How well do you take care of yourself physically? Identify three activities that you currently do and/or plan to engage in from this point forward to take care of yourself physically.

A.

B.

C.

2. Emotional Self-Care:
The things I do to take care of my feelings in healthy ways. Examples include: maintaining personal and professional support systems; counseling and/or therapy as needed; journaling; and talking about feelings in healthy ways. How well do you take care of yourself emotionally? Identify three activities that you currently do and/or plan to engage in from this point forward to take care of yourself emotionally.

A.

B.

C.

Happy Teacher Revolution:
The Educator's Roadmap to Claiming & Sustaining Joy

(Continued)

Figure P2.1

3. Cognitive Self-Care

The things I do to take care of my mind and understand myself better. Examples include: reading for pleasure or work; writing; and engaging in continued education for additional knowledge/skill. How well do you take care of yourself psychologically? Identify three activities that you currently do and/or plan to engage in from this point forward to take care of yourself psychologically.

A.

B.

C.

4. Social Self-Care:

The things I do in relation to others and the world around me. Examples include: spending time with friends, family and colleagues you enjoy; having fun and playing; belonging to groups, communities and activities that encourage positive social connections. How well do you take care of yourself socially? Identify three activities that you currently do and/or plan to engage in from this point forward to take care of yourself socially.

A.

B.

C.

5. Financial Self-Care:

The things I do to spend and save responsibly. Examples include: balancing a checking account; planning for the future; and spending money in thoughtful and productive ways. How well do you take care of yourself financially? Identify three activities that you currently do and/or plan to engage in from this point forward to take care of yourself financially.

A.

B.

C.

Figure P2.1a (Continued)

6. Spiritual Self-Care

The things I do to gain perspective on my life. Examples include: prayer; meditation; contact with nature; participating in worship with a community, and music. How well do you take care of yourself spiritually? Identify three activities that you currently do and/or plan to engage in from this point forward to take care of yourself spiritually.

A.

B.

C.

Now you've read the checklist and made a list of strategies for yourself. That is not enough. The bottom line is that self-care requires a conscious effort to practice individual wellness strategies on a regular basis. If we are able to make a commitment to do so both personally and professionally, we can prevent the negative consequences of compassion fatigue and stay well on the journey to student success.

Worksheets from *Making Professional Wellness a Priority!* by Mona M. Johnson, 2002 and US Department of Education

Happy Teacher Revolution:
The Educator's Roadmap to Claiming & Sustaining Joy

Figure P2.1 (Continued)

GUIDED MEDITATION: CULTIVATING JOY AND CONNECTION WITH SELF

By Elayne Mendoza

VIDEO P2.1

Elayne narrates a guided meditation with written text included below for you to consider deepening your connection with yourself.

https://www.wiley.com/go/happyteacherrevolution

Take this opportunity to pause and enter the present moment wherever you are right now.

I am going to take you on a journey toward cultivating joy within self. So start by gently closing your eyes, sensing the body, and observing how you are feeling right now.

Wherever you are, whether that is at your desk, inside of your car, or in the comfort of your home, start to feel the surface beneath you, lengthen your spine, and relax your shoulders.

Now focus on your breathing, and begin by slowly inhaling through your nose and exhaling through your nose

Inhale.

Exhale.

Deep breath in and deep breath out.

One more, in through the nose and out through the nose.

And as you continue to breathe, take this moment as an opportunity to think of one thing about yourself that brings you joy. Perhaps this is a quality in you that others have always complimented you on. Or perhaps it's a comment that you heard frequently from students.

From those you lead and teach.

Bring this one thing to your attention and notice the sensations that arise inside of your body.

How do you feel when you receive these compliments from other people? Are you happy, appreciative, joyful, or at peace?

Once the feeling has been discovered. Take note of how your body's internal sensations change and intensify.

Feel this emotion deeply anchored into your body.

And now take a deep breath in and exhale, sigh it out.

Feel this sensation spreading outward from your heart, and have faith that when you experience these emotions in your body the people around you will also feel them.

And trust that these feelings are available to you at any time throughout the day.

And now, before you return back to your day. Take a moment to focus on your breathing once more and breathe deeply through your nose and then let all the air out of your lungs

Exhale and fully, fully release.

And now pause.

Open your eyes slowly and softly, move your toes and your fingers

Return back to reality and lead with love.

Somatic Embodiment Experience

Video P2.2

Maya Basik, former educator and embodiment teacher, guides us through an opportunity to be present in the physical body. Consider participating in this embodiment practice to support you in cultivating joy within yourself and holding that joy sustainably in a safe, relaxed, and grounded body system.

https://www.wiley.com/go/happyteacherrevolution

Breathing Experience

Video P2.3

Keith Golden, musician and movement teacher, guides us through a straightforward box breathing experience to drop us into our bodies and breath.

https://www.wiley.com/go/happyteacherrevolution

Scent Experience

A good jumping-off point when working with your connection with the self and scent, suggested by expert Theresa Cangialosi, is noting what smell you're drawn to. The body knows this instinctively, and when you get more familiar with different scents, you may be drawn to something more calming or perhaps a different energy. *Safety note: Many essential oils are toxic to pets, and please do not ingest any essential oils.*

Suggested scent example for deepening connection within the self: *Eucalyptus (Eucalyptus radiata)*

Soundtrack Experience

Additional music suggestions are available for your listening enjoyment on the official Happy Teacher Revolution Playlist on Spotify.

"It Gets Better" by GRiZ, DRAM
"That I Would Be Good" by Alanis Morisette, Christopher Fogel
"Rise Up" by Andra Day

Taste Experience

Danna Banana Golden Smoothie

This breakfast smoothie is my go-to in warmer months when I have a craving for Golden Milk. It can include frozen mango, as detailed here, or extra frozen banana is delicious, too!

¼ cup milk of your choice
1 sliced frozen banana (slice a ripened banana before freezing so it's easier for your blender)
1 cup frozen mango (optional)
½ cup yogurt of your choice (I use full-fat Greek but it's up to you)
½–1 teaspoon turmeric powder (or Golden Milk powder, available in some stores)
Optional: pinch of black pepper
Optional: 1 teaspoon Ashwagandha powder
Optional: 1 scoop vanilla protein powder

Optional: sweeten to taste with 1 tablespoon agave nectar or maple syrup

Add everything to a blender and mix until smooth. Top with bee pollen, chia seeds, or nothing at all!

DANNA BANANA PUMPKIN SMOOTHIE

I love this breakfast smoothie in the cooler months to substitute for any pumpkin spice–flavored drink. Did you know that a very famous coffee chain's "pumpkin spice" doesn't contain any actual pumpkin, just lots of sugar and additives to mimic a pumpkin taste? This is a healthier alternative and absolutely delicious. Top with pumpkin seeds, granola, and/or a dusting of the pumpkin pie spice.

½ cup pumpkin purée (canned)
¼ cup milk of your choice (I use almond oat or milk)
1 sliced frozen banana
½ cup yogurt of your choice (I use Greek)
1 teaspoon maple syrup (or to taste)
1 tablespoon cashew butter or almond butter
½ teaspoon of pumpkin pie spice (or ⅛ teaspoon ground nutmeg, ⅛ teaspoon ground ginger, ⅛ teaspoon ground cloves, and ⅛ teaspoon ground cinnamon)
Optional Protein Powder (I use 1 scoop vanilla)

Add everything to a blender and mix until smooth. Top with chia seeds, pumpkin seeds, granola, or nothing at all!

OVERNIGHT OATS

I love to prep this the night before in a Mason jar to take with me on the go. You can also top your overnight oats with granola, cacao nibs, bee pollen, fresh fruit, slivered almonds or other nuts, or nothing at all! Sometimes I also stir in full-fat Greek yogurt for some protein and fat, but that's up to you.

½ cup old-fashioned oats
½ cup milk of your choice
½ teaspoon maple syrup
¼ teaspoon pure vanilla extract

I like to let this sit for a few minutes and then shake all ingredients in the Mason jar before refrigerating overnight (or at least 6 hours). It keeps for up to 4 days.

POETRY EXPERIENCE

Dear Miss Thomas

I like school
And writing about the spooky witch
Who works at Burger King
And has long fingernails
Because
It makes me happy
When you take a thumbtack
And post my story
On the bulletin board
Behind your desk.
But I'm scared
To tell you something sad
Because I know you like to smile
When I tell you about my weekend
In my daily journal.
My uncle died
Yesterday

And I came to school
Today
And I'll be here
Tomorrow.
But no one knows
He was shot.
I'm upset
Miss Thomas
That my uncle
Never got to read
The Spooky Witch.

I Stand

white smocked
in line
for my school picture,
as my kindergarten teacher
hopelessly attempts
to comb out
my matted hair
I constantly
chew on.
Tilting her head to the left,
she says
sometimes
there are the knots
that just don't come out
and I feel her shove me
onto the stool,
demanding a smile
aimed at the lens.

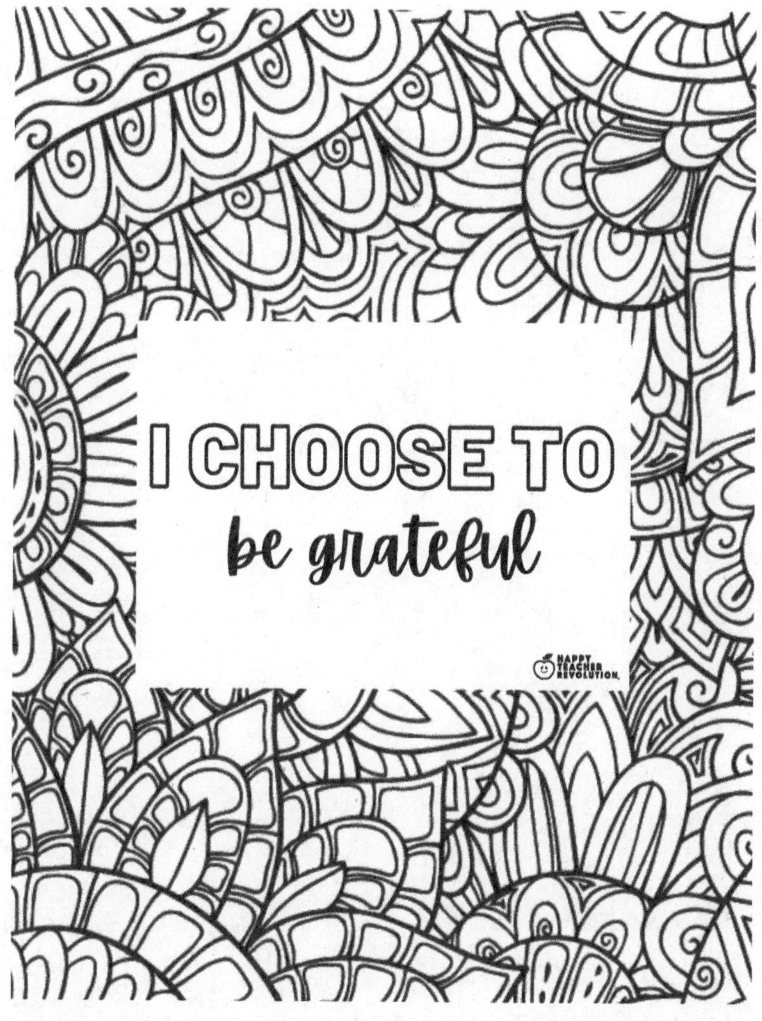

Figure P2.2

PART III

Nurturing Relationships with Colleagues, Families, and Kids

Self-care is community.

—Lynn Harper, Instructional Support Specialist, Illinois

We can move mountains through relationships. Relationships have a transformative neurobiological power, and more research points to the power of community than ever before. Specifically, our nervous system plays an important role in the safety we find within relationships. This is called the social engagement system. The science behind the social nervous system has helped us to better understand the importance of coregulation with one another. This part of the nervous system was completely unstudied and pretty much unknown until the 1990s when Stephen Porges's research described the polyvagal theory and completely shifted how we understand and work with the nervous system and its connection to relationships via neuroscience (Johnson, 2021). Our bodies and nervous systems are designed to connect with others, and positive relationships are absolutely essential to our well-being.

It was through my connections with other teachers that the Happy Teacher Revolution Movement was born. During the year I taught the largest class of kindergarteners over the course of my classroom career, 39 to be exact, I felt called to create a grassroots support structure not only for my colleagues in the profession but also for myself. I was teaching in a toxic school environment, one that was not just physically toxic in terms of the asbestos in the tiles or lead in the water or mice droppings in the teachers' lounge, but emotionally toxic as well.

> *Until the day we die, we long for safe and reliable connections. Co-regulation is essential; first for survival and then for living a life of well-being.*
>
> —Deb Dana, LCSW, *Anchored: How to Befriend Your Nervous System Using Polyvagal Theory* (Sounds True, 2021, p. 40)

Dehumanization, and the loss of connection with one another, happens when we don't see or hear each other in the smallest interaction or on the largest scale. Educators, especially, have resonance when it comes to these interpersonal interactions. Our energy is palpable to those around us. If an educator standing over class is resonating as peaceful, notice if there is a shift in the class being peaceful. If an educator resonating frustration is in charge, the shift is palpable in frustrated vibes from the students. In order to lead as your authentic self, both in terms of leading students and also leading colleagues, you have to come *from* a deeper place to go *to* a deeper place. Nurturing relationships among others is rooted in self-cultivation and transformation.

Burnout begins when we forget our purpose, and it only deepens when we lose track of ourselves and of each other and our sense of belonging within the larger community. The healing we must actively engage in, both as individuals and through the power of community, is the vehicle through which we can enact systemic change. We cannot be unhealed healers in the midst of this work. Our spirits and sense of self cannot be in deficit in doing this work.

> *It doesn't matter whether you talk to people who work in social justice and mental health and abuse and neglect, what we know is that connection, the ability to feel connected, is—neurobiologically that's how we're wired—it's why we're here.*
>
> —Brené Brown, "The Power of Vulnerability" (2010b)

7

Modeling and Building Community

Relationships are roots. Our roots keep us tethered to Mother Earth and help us weather storms that may come our way with flexibility and strength. Kindness, compassion, and empathy aren't like slices of a pie that, once doled out to yourself, your loved ones, your friends, your students, nothing remains for your colleagues or complete strangers. When you hold yourself with kindness and compassion, you are able to continue giving.

It may feel easier to insulate than to reach out. Some background thoughts in my brain that have run on repeat sound like: "They don't care. They aren't shutting me out . . . but they act like I don't exist. Like I'm not there." This feeling of invisibility and feelings of rejection are the opposite of belonging. I start to wonder whether, if I disappeared, anyone would notice; would my replacement be hired so quickly that I would be completely forgotten in the blink of an eye? This realization of my replaceability also made me aware that no amount of investment in indulgencies or the inherent privilege embedded within the self-care industry could negate feelings of isolation, invisibility, rejection, and abandonment. "What capitalism, patriarchy, and white supremacy want you to believe is that you don't have a responsibility to think deeply about your existence. It prioritizes self-optimization at the expense of community wellness" (Róisín, 2022, pp. 54–55).

When I was first grappling with symptoms associated with anxiety and depression, I felt alone not only with my feelings but also alone in the greater sense that no one else out there could possibly understand. One of the most compelling moments of my personal healing journey after I was "officially diagnosed" was stumbling upon online groups of people who also were experiencing depression. As I read their stories, they put words to sentiments I hadn't been able to do previously and made me feel a sense of belonging within the depths of this isolating loneliness. A layer of shame was removed as I started to see light peeking through.

Similarly, when I started teaching, I realized that while we were surrounded by humans all day long, we still didn't have the opportunity to connect with fellow adults from a social-emotional standpoint. My colleagues were facing similar challenges relating to the profession, and yet we were siloed into our individual classrooms within our own set of four walls enclosing us from the opportunity to connect organically. Outside of back-to-school icebreaker activities or the occasional work happy hour, there truly were few opportunities to share our authentic selves with one another. Happy Teacher Revolution developed out of a desperate need to foster the social-emotional learning of adults when regarding self-awareness, social awareness, and relationship skills.

I believe the best social-emotional learning curriculum for our students is actually the *adults* in that child's life modeling social-emotional competencies like the ones just mentioned. Our students are astute and pick up on subtle cues regarding social-emotional relationship competencies. Trauma-informed pedagogy is just as much about the adult as it is about the student. We have the unique opportunity to reconsider what professional development spaces look like in terms of fostering humanity with one another as an essential part of the foundational pedagogy.

Positive Relations with Others

A healthy community is a healing community, and a healing community is full of hope because it has seen its own people weather—survive and thrive.
—Bruce D. Perry and Oprah Winfrey, *What Happened to You? Conversations on Trauma, Resilience, and Healing* (2021, p. 203)

CREATE SPACE TO FOSTER CONNECTION

The more we can get together and dig deep . . . that's where the magic really happens.

—Karina Vergara, former Educator and Education Specialist, South Texas

VIDEO 7.1

Karina recommends creating a sense of community, whether in person or digitally, to connect in a group chat. She also encourages educators to connect in communities like Happy Teacher Revolution to foster authentic human connection.

https://www.wiley.com/go/happyteacherrevolution

Self-care is relational care. Self-care is community care. I started Happy Teacher Revolution because my essential question was this: How might we create time and space for teachers to feel, deal, and be real about the social-emotional and intellectual demands of the job? My solution was to revolutionize well-being by not focusing only on the individual through the lens of self-care but by also including the collective through the lens of community care.

"Remember the ability to find more purpose in your work begins by becoming more purposeful in the way you interact with *people*. It's about living aligned with your values and expressing yourself at that level" (O'Brien, 2022, p. 199). One of the values that was important in founding Happy Teacher Revolution was creating a space to amplify voices that have been silenced, to hold space for one another, and to give visibility for those who haven't been invited to have a seat at the proverbial table. The groups offer spaces for collective care and individual care, but not necessarily from a judgmental point of view. In the groups, individuals arrive at their own self-discoveries from a place of self-compassion; they also bear witness to the authenticity of others.

Join the Revolution by getting certified to facilitate community spaces through the Happy Teacher Revolution Framework. School administrators can support connection among staff by creating opportunities to foster adult social-emotional learning like those Happy Teacher

Join the Revolution.

Revolution offers. Our pilot sites have seen profound results when administrators view staff well-being as a worthwhile and ongoing professional development opportunity. Prioritizing well-being supports and including them as part of the contractual workday demonstrates that leadership compassionately views their staff as human beings. Teachers who are passionate about wellness, compassion, empathy, and connection in addressing issues of burnout can become certified through our programming opportunities and hold their own Happy Teacher Revolution meetings in their school, district, or city. I have held meetings that are school based and also open meetings in the Baltimore community for any teacher to attend, regardless of their school location. To get certified to start a meeting in your area, check out www.HappyTeacherRevolution.com.

Create and seek community.

If you're feeling lonely or craving community, find fun stuff to try. Bonus points if it's free. For me, fun stuff includes book exchange meetups at my local bookstore, free community yoga, or becoming a regular at my favorite local tea shop. Engaging socially in digital spaces can also be helpful, whether it's through Mighty Networks, Meetup, Teachers Connect, or our own Happy Teacher Revolution online community meetings.

VALUE COLLABORATION OVER COMPETITION

> *Replace comparison with collaboration and use the teaching community as inspiration to grow, develop, and improve your abilities as an educator. When teachers join forces, embrace their differences, and advance together, the entire field of education benefits.*
>
> —Michelle Emerson, *First Class Teaching: 10 Lessons You Don't Learn in College* (2023, p. 150)

I started my teaching journey in Southeast Asia teaching conversational English in an orphanage and sustainable school. Helping one another to solve problems and supporting one another toward a common goal was culturally acceptable, even encouraged. This level of collaboration was fostered in people at a very young age, which meant that when I gave a quiz or tried to assess my students' understanding of concepts I had taught, this collaborative mindset actually "looked" and "sounded" like cheating from my point of view. In reality, this was a conscious choice of collaboration.

We can view each other as competition or embrace one another in community. When we are able to collaborate rather than being in silos within the four walls of our individual spaces, we become less like islands and more like networks. Collaborating is like a potluck dinner: Each individual contributes a dish rather than one person providing everything.

When it comes to workplace well-being, "leaders should be able to increase the satisfaction of individuals with a relatively powerless or low-level job by giving them a greater perception of choice, thereby increasing autonomy" (Rock and Cox, 2012, p. 6).

Autonomy

In fact:

> Employees with a greater sense of autonomy reported greater job satisfaction and reduced anxiety. Social neuroscience research highlights the cognitive and neural mechanisms underlying this phenomenon—since the perception of autonomy is processed in the brain as a reward, and that fostering intrinsic motivation is also rewarding, implementing leadership practices that increase autonomy and intrinsic motivation in employees will increase productivity and promote collaboration. (Rock and Cox, 2012, p. 6)

Have an actual potluck.

One way to foster community, be present in the body, and facilitate connection is by hosting a potluck. One Happy Teacher Revolutionary started integrating breakfast potlucks as a way to gather for Happy Teacher Revolution meetings. Picture a sundae bar, but instead it's an assemble-your-own-breakfast-yogurt-parfait-type station: fresh fruits, granola, nuts, whatever! Consider integrating opportunities to bring visibility to the type of collaboration evident in your community while also integrating nutritious opportunities to support your well-being.

PRACTICE "UNMASKING"

Having that support and genuine concern from my principal encouraged me to take better care of myself and realize that my school community can be a source of support for things going on both in and outside of the building. I tried too hard to separate my teacher-self from my whole self, and my principal helped me realize that we are all just people with vulnerabilities and there is no shame in needing support.

—Rachel McGrain, former Music Education Teacher, Baltimore, Maryland

Being able to take the mask off and share that you are a human being first before you are your job title is absolutely terrifying. This sharing can feel even scarier when it is within connection with someone who is in a position of power or authority, whether formal or informal. In this practice of unmasking yourself, be mindful around who you are choosing to be authentic with. Before possibly oversharing your thoughts or feelings, invite the consent of the individual to whom you are considering sharing your truth. This component of consent is important so that you can discern who is open and available to hold space for you and who may not be able or ready to receive you at this time.

> *Share something about yourself outside of your job description.*

Bring a component of your "whole self" to the community you are in. Whether it is sharing a hobby or activity you do outside of work, a podcast or book you've been into recently, or a part of your culture or family tradition, take a moment to take the mask off of your identity in your professional role. Consider making the vulnerable act of introducing a part of who you are that may be new to your community.

> *If you take the mask off and people get the "ick," maybe those aren't your people.*

It's important to be discerning and intentional around who you choose to be vulnerable with. You get to decide how to titrate this vulnerability with others so that it feels safe. Just as in chemistry, we can titrate this vulnerability so that it doesn't feel like too much, too fast, too soon. You have the sovereignty to decide if you share and how much you choose to share in both in-person and virtual connections.

Social media is made for consumption . . . and, as humans, we aren't made for consumption. We are made for *connection*. If there are individuals who do not align with you and your values (digitally and/or in person), they are not your people. The more we can model this "unmasking," the more we will clear out those who do not align and continue building connections with those who do.

Surround yourself with people who align to your authenticity, people who make you realize there's nothing wrong with being who you are. Be discerning in who you share your vulnerabilities with. When you are living in your truth, you not only provide visibility and inspiration to others in what that authenticity looks like in action, but it also provides an opportunity to foster community. In this way, each of the members within the community employs their individual talents to serve the collective whole by sharing their authentic gifts with the world.

CONSENT TO VENT

> *To help support my own esteem, I vent to someone I trust. I have to remind myself I am a good teacher and I'm doing a great job and that's enough. Because if I just keep comparing myself to the Pinterest-perfect teacher on social media, I think I would quit if I was just trying to keep up with that persona and be just like her.*
>
> —Elizabeth M., Early Childhood Teacher, Baltimore, Maryland

I invite you to consider holding a period of time to be your authentic, uncensored self. Schedule a time to vent. It's important to receive permission to vent from the person you are engaging with rather than just dumping on them. They may not be able to receive you, and consent is an important step. If you want to ask someone to listen to you vent, first ask if they are able to hold space for you right now. Sometimes we don't want people to fix or solve the issue for us, we just want to share what is weighing on us. We want to feel heard, seen, understood. Again, it is important to ask for consent before venting. Perhaps say: "I want to share something that's been weighing on me. This isn't personal and it is not yours to hold. I simply want to share and verbalize myself without taking action." Compartmentalizing the vent session is just like a faucet: You can turn it on and turn it off, and then it is OFF. "Share your frustrations with someone who will sympathize but who will also encourage you to overcome obstacles. In other words, venting about your job is not the same thing as wallowing in negativity or ignoring ways you can prompt change" (Rankin 2017, p. 14).

Make complaining effective and adaptive.

The most common question I get from leaders about Happy Teacher Revolution meetings is if they are just random b!*#-fests. I often respond that any professional development session has the potential to turn into hours of complaining, and if we had the opportunity to give educators a constructive time and space to vent, doing so may be incredibly effective. According to Whitney Goodman (2023), prominent researchers who study complaining behavior found that those who complain with the hopes of achieving a certain result tend to the happier. Complaining serves an important purpose in our lives.

EIGHT TIPS FOR EFFECTIVE COMPLAINING

1. *Figure out the complaint. What is really bothering you?*
2. *Identify the goal.*
   (a) *Are you trying to make someone aware of an issue?*
   (b) *Do you want to enact change?*
   (c) *Do you want to be heard?*
   (d) *Do you want to be validated?*
   (e) *Do you want advice?*
3. *Choose the right audience. Who can help [you with this]? Is there anyone who would understand or relate? Don't always complain to the same people. Pick people who can actually validate you or help you with your goal.*
4. *Decide if it's worth it. Think about the issues that are* really *important to you, and complain in moderation.*
   (a) *What will happen if [you do] complain about this?*
   (b) *What will happen if [you] don't complain about this?*

5. *Validate that you may want to complain because you're looking for connection. Is there anything else you can share to connect through something* other *than a complaint?*
6. *Write it down. [This can be especially helpful if you feel like it's hard to manage your complaints.] Research shows that writing helps [focus and] organize experiences and leads to greater understanding of what happened and how to cope.*
7. *Be as direct about your issue as possible.*
8. *Remember that there are real inequities in the world. [People may call you "negative" or "complainer" for bringing up the inequities in the world. There are people who have it worse. Keep talking about the issue and focus on your goal.]*

Source: Whitney Goodman, *Toxic Positivity: Keeping It Real in a World Obsessed with Being Happy* (Orion Spring, 2022), pp. 187–188. Reproduced with permission.

The goal here is not to swallow down your complaints, pretend that everything is fine, and/or eliminate complaining from your life altogether. Rather, consider these eight helpful tips and notice when your complaining becomes more specific and goal oriented rather than a seemingly endless loop.

FIND A POLYVAGAL PARTNER

The science and safety of connection is growing each day, and our understanding of how the nervous system works continues to deepen. While learning about the nervous system can at times feel very scientific, understanding our biology actually opens us up to the mystery and magic of life.

—Deb Dana, *Anchored: How to Befriend Your Nervous System Using Polyvagal Theory* (Sounds True, 2021, p. 195)

We are built for connection and hardwired to seek meaningful connection. When we tune in to ourselves to befriend our nervous system and tend to our own well-being through the methods suggested in the first section of this book, we open the realm of opportunities and limitless possibilities of supporting our own personal growth. It is through this expansiveness that we can magnify our experiences by sharing our journey of personal growth with others.

Based on research in neuroscience,

> we know that our nervous system looks for, and longs for, connection. Throughout our lives we search for opportunities to coregulate. We receive great physical and psychological benefits from befriending our nervous system and learning to anchor ourselves and our bodies in regulation. When we share our experiences with others, the benefits magnify. To support our autonomic movement toward well-being, it's helpful to have people in our lives who are willing to share the journey with us. (Dana, 2021, p. 170)

A good place to begin is with what Dana describes as a polyvagal partner. This partner is someone

> who will help you see what's changing and hear your new stories and who wants you to help them see how they are shaping new pathways as well. Inviting someone to be a polyvagal partner is an opportunity to share what you've learned about your nervous system and help a friend begin to befriend their nervous system. (2021, p. 171)

When we invite someone into exploring these new learnings, we are opening the window of possibility to deepen our understanding of ourselves, as well. Consider this "an invitation to experience deep listening and the intimacy that emerges from being in connection" (ibid.). We discuss polyvagal theory more in Chapter 14, but for now, consider this an invitation to find safety in your nervous system through the process of coregulation via a polyvagal partner. By connecting with another person to both mindfully listen and mindfully share with one another, you have the opportunity to model and build community through deepening human connection.

Positive Relations with Others

Dana shares that our individual beliefs about self-care are influenced by the people and places that are a

---

Initiate a microcommunity.

---

part of our daily lives. Consider where you work, who you're surrounded by, and what your environment entails. Do people around you encourage you to practice self-care, or do they think self-care is unimportant? Do you live in a place where it's easy to practice self-care? Do you work in a place that encourages self-care? If we're surrounded by people who have a rigid view of self-care and live and work in places that don't value self-care, we may find it harder to hear and follow our own needs.

When we're surrounded by individuals who encourage self-care and live and work in places that value self-care, we find it easier to attend to self-care and create practices that nourish our nervous system (Dana, 2021). It has been said that you are the company you keep. In case you can't do a total life overhaul at the moment, consider having just a few individuals comprise your microcommunity. Jot those names down in the margin here and sticky-tab this page. Refer to it when you feel dysregulated and/or crave to connect with someone who also understands the nervous system and is prioritizing their own journey of well-being.

Deepening connection and understanding with yourself while simultaneously reprogramming your body within a sense of safety is a profoundly powerful experience to foster authentic community connection. Check out the Happy Teacher Revolution curriculum available at www.HappyTeacherRevolution.com. You can launch an evidence-based practice within your own community by getting certified as a Happy Teacher Revolutionary.

8

Offering and Requesting Meaningful Appreciation

Teacher Appreciation Week has been a sore subject for me for a number of years. I honestly thought I was actually cursed during that week. One year my purse was stolen out of my classroom. Another year I got dumped. Another year I had to sit in a district court for a former administrator who sexually harassed multiple staff members and ended up being voted not guilty unanimously by the jury. Then I got dumped a second time by someone else. All these events occurred during the one week of the year where I was supposed to be the most appreciated, or so I thought. Well, as it turns out, I began to realize that maybe the invitation was for me to consider how each of these upheavals was an opportunity to appreciate the shadows as much as the light. They also were moments for me to recognize that perhaps we are not setting ourselves up for success by prioritizing just one week of the year for appreciation; rather we should integrate this sentiment throughout the entirety of the year.

When it comes to appreciation, I've realized that it starts with recognizing the importance of prioritizing a sense of appreciation for oneself. Consider actively showing appreciation for the "good" qualities that are celebrated in our culture and also appreciating your shadows, too: grief, rage, anger, sadness, anxiety. We can start honoring and celebrating the full spectrum of emotions and aspects of ourselves through a lens of appreciation, then echo the practice outward to others. Once you feel held and supported yourself, you can operate from that place to offer meaningful appreciation for those around you; Because there is quite a backlash type of scenario when there is inauthentic appreciation that everyone can sense is far from genuine.

Speaking of inauthenticity, it's about time I name the plague sweeping the world of education: toxic positivity. The phrase "toxic positivity" resonates with so many of us because it is a way to respond to yourself or to others that lacks empathy and is dismissive of emotions.

> When we show up authentically, rather than using toxic positivity, we're validating that act the other person is going through is real, empathizing, and not sugarcoating or denying their experience. You may not totally agree with how they're handling it or their interpretation of the situation, but you're authentically trying to connect and show up for them. You're saying that you hear them by sitting with them and allowing them to show up fully (in a safe way that doesn't violate your boundaries, of course). (Goodman, 2022, p. 17).

When it comes to meaningful appreciation, it can be helpful to distinguish between toxic positivity and helpful positivity. In her book *Toxic Positivity*, Whitney Goodman writes how toxic positivity is all around us—but it's important that we don't view everything happy or positive as toxic. Remember, positivity isn't inherently toxic; it *becomes* toxic.

The following are all examples of toxic positivity: when someone

> Tells people they shouldn't be feeling what they're feeling; implies that people are negative if they can't find the silver lining in everything; encourages people to be happy all the time and always see the "good";

> ends the conversation or relationship because [they] don't want any "negativity" or "bad vibes"; uses phrases or statement that diminish what the person is experiencing in an attempt to help them "feel better" or "get over it"; only looks out for the "good" and ignores anything "bad"; shames people for having bad days or negative moments.

Someone engaging in helpful positivity, in contrast:

> Recognizes the value of seeing the good and allows people to arrive at their own beneficial conclusions and to take their time getting there; recognizes that humans have a variety of emotions, some more challenging than others, and allows people to see the "good" and "bad" sides of a situation; has an understanding that not all situations have a silver lining and we will still experience joy; encourages emotional expression from others (with boundaries) and from within ourselves, knowing that for some to experience happiness, they often have to process and move through the pain; [and] looks out for and recognizes the highs and lows of a situation. (Goodman, 2022, pp. 272–273)

The next sections offer support around facilitating meaningful appreciation to others and teaching others how to provide you meaningful appreciation, as well.

CULTIVATE GRATITUDE

The practice of gratitude helps me stay in a clear, open, spacious, positive mindset. And it also deepens the connection that I feel with the people around me and with the world around me.

—Ashley Williams, former Educator and Founder of Clymb, an organization to support student social-emotional learning

VIDEO 8.1

In this video, Ashley shares her practice of gratitude as a means of showing appreciation toward self and others and describes the implications of this important ritual.

https://www.wiley.com/go/happyteacherrevolution

Gratitude is an appreciation for what we consider valuable. Gratitude is an action, an embodied feeling, and tied to the ventral vagal system. "Physically, as we enter a moment of gratitude, our heart rhythms change, our blood pressure drops, our immune function improves, our stress is reduced, and we sleep longer and deeper. Psychologically, we feel more joyful, more alive, more generous, more satisfaction, and less burnout" (Dana, 2021, p. 169).

As Ashley shared, gratitude doesn't require a huge time commitment or elaborate ritual. During her morning routine, Principal Jessica Cabeen writes down three people she was grateful for the day before and why.

> During the school year, I have challenged myself to intentionally recognize every staff member in the building by sending a card home with a specific word of gratitude. I make a point of stopping and giving positive praise to students daily. While all of this can be seen to establish and maintain a healthy school culture, I see it as a way to maintain my sanity and see the good in any situation, even the really bad ones. (Cabeen, 2023, p. 27)

According to Goodman (2022): "Recent research does demonstrate that a regular gratitude practice moderately benefits mental well-being, emotional well-being, and social well-being. Evidence shows that gratitude interventions like journaling, when done regularly, do improve emotional well-being" (p. 132). This makes complete sense as we orient ourselves toward what's good in our lives. When we are able to name the parts of life that we are grateful for, we not only feel more in control but we also have positive emotions about ourselves. If we only focus on what isn't working or what is outside our control, we feel worse. The goal here is to be able to hold both the gratitude as well as the acknowledgment that there are still challenging moments, too. As researchers Emily Nagoski and Amelia Nagoski stress in their book *Burnout: The Secret to Unlocking the Stress Cycle*: "Being grateful for good things doesn't erase the difficult things" (2020, p. 208). Rather, gratitude helps us hold the both/and as we experience the full spectrum of human emotions.

Gratitude can take many forms. The emphasis here is choosing your own gratitude adventure that aligns with you. Is it writing a note? Sending a text or voice note? Making a phone call? Sending silent intentional gratitude during morning meditation? Is it writing three things you're grateful for at the beginning of or end of the day? Is it all the above or something completely different?

Design your own gratitude practice.

There's a multitude of ways to engage with gratitude throughout your day. Just remember, gratitude cannot exist without validation and emotional processing. "Before you use any of these gratitude-enhancing skills, it's important to make sure that you're in a place where you're ready to receive and experience gratitude. If you move too quickly it will probably feel forced and unhelpful" (Goodman, 2022, p. 137). Here are some habits Goodman suggests that you consider as a regular gratitude practice:

- Pay attention to and recognize both the good and bad in your life. It usually helps to start with the parts you're struggling with most and then go for gratitude.
- Write down the things that you are grateful for. You can journal about a particular topic, make a list, draw a picture, or do anything that orients your attention to the feeling of gratitude.
- Say thank you and acknowledge people. It feels really good to help others and this also improves our social bonds. Make it a point to say thank you, smile, and compliment others.

> . . . The more you're able to validate your feelings, solve problems effectively, and develop perspective, the more likely you are to develop a consistent state of gratitude. The most important part of cultivating gratitude is doing it regularly and not just in moments of struggle. (Goodman, 2022, pp. 137–138)

I did this every school year, and found the practice to be incredibly helpful in relationship building. Within the first week of school, I tried to make a phone call to every home for every student to introduce myself and share one great thing about their student that I appreciated so far. Doing this builds positive rapport and also helps you as a teacher to have an example in your brain of something you

Start the year with an appreciation message.

appreciate or value about this child. While it may not be possible to replicate this exact practice, consider sending notes of appreciation to your community at the beginning of the school year, calendar year, seasonal shifts, or whatever timeline works in order to implement a practice of calling out appreciation in another.

CONSIDER "CODE LAVENDER"

"Code Lavender" is a way to provide ongoing support and ensure that caring for our caregivers is, and always will be, central to our success.

—Carol Gomes, Chief Executive Officer of Stony Brook University Hospital

In a hospital, the term "code" describes something that needs urgent attention. In the world of healthcare, a multitude of codes signify different events—"Code Red" for fire or "Code Blue" for medical emergencies, to name a few. Two hospitals in Cleveland and Hawaii have introduced a new code: "Code Lavender." This signals that the need is urgent, but the goal is to try to bring some calming influence to a painful or stressful situation.

Code Lavender addresses stress and burnout by providing holistic rapid responses to colleagues who are facing emotionally stressful events. The members of the Code Lavender team (fellow nurses at the hospital) arrive with water, aromatherapy lotions, healthy snacks, relaxing music and the message—loud and clear: "You matter . . . and what you just went through matters. Take a breather . . . we're here for you."

As Carol Gomes explained, as part of the process, nurses gave out lavender wrist bands to anyone who wanted one—to remind them to go a little easy on themselves for a while. Sometimes folks didn't even want to stop—they just grabbed the bracelet and a hug.

The code itself can include very little conversation and contact or longer conversations as needed by the persons involved. Responders can listen or just sit in silence with those who need to know that they can talk if they need to, tell stories of the incident, relate memories of the beloved coworker or patient, or let off some steam. The code allows some small space for us to breathe and take comfort from each other.

When employees feel supported by the institution they work for, they experience less burnout, higher satisfaction, take fewer sick days, and have better interactions with others. Those we serve and support receive better care and have a better overall experience if their caregivers have more to give. Caring plus caring seems to add up to even more caring, not any less (2019).

Code Lavender and other holistic support services show us the interconnectedness between the student/family/staff ecosystem. All benefit when we consider this interdependence, when one part of the whole is nourished and supported.

Integrate a system around community care (even if it is a low-level intervention).

In your school setting, think about how to incorporate components of Code Lavender on your team or on your floor. At my school, one day we called a Code Lavender for an Early Childhood teacher who had had a traumatic experience the day before. We incorporated her morning-block students into our classes so she could have a moment of peace.

Many holistic wellness providers, such as chiropractors and massage therapists, offer pro bono services to caregivers. Wellness providers in training, as in schools of massage, are required to collect practicum hours and are able to offer services free of charge. My team has also made a Sunshine Basket for a team member who was consumed with worry and grief because a family member was missing. Consider incorporating components of Code Lavender within your school community to foster compassion and connection.

Purpose in Life

KNOW YOUR "WHY"

Know your WHY—why do you want to work with students, with this age group—because that helps drive you. Teachers are not shy about hard work. We start getting burnt out when we start getting beat down and not recognized or appreciated.

—Nancy Ynchaustegui, Seventh- and Eighth-Grade Science Teacher, Union, New Jersey

https://www.wiley.com/go/happyteacherrevolution

VIDEO 8.2

Nancy was Teacher of the Year 2020 in her school. Go, Nancy!!! Unfortunately, she didn't receive a single email recognizing her achievement, and she did not get to celebrate with her students. In this video, Nancy describes the importance in knowing your "why" as a supportive practice in fostering your purpose in life.

Sometimes the appreciation piece does not look or sound like what we actually deserve. And that can feel brutal. But consider an invitation to drop into your own truth, your own knowing, your own WHY behind the work. According to Anthony Burrow, a developmental psychologist and director of the Purpose and Identity Processes Laboratory at Cornell University, people who feel a sense of purpose in their lives may be better able to handle daily stress and regulate their emotions (Bronfenbrenner Center for Translational Research, 2019). If you can appreciate and name the reason why you are doing this important work, you are cultivating a sense of appreciation that emanates outward like a ripple effect on everyone who surrounds you.

Make a "spark joy" collection.

Compile an album in your phone or print out/physically keep a binder of quotes, photos of individuals who inspire you, and any art/music/creations that inspire you to consider a greater sense of self—a spark joy collection, if you will, inspired by Marie Kondo, the world-renowned tidying expert who declutters by prioritizing joy. I have a wall of photos of individuals who have impacted my road to where I am today. Intermixed with photos of Michelle Obama and Frida Kahlo are photos with my heroes whom I've had the incredible opportunity to meet in real life, including Chris Emdin, Valencia Clay, and Angela Watson. This wall also contains screenshots of emails, texts, and DMs of individuals who have affirmed the Happy Teacher Revolution and represent light that I want to imbue my space, even if subconsciously.

Build and cultivate appreciation for community with the earth/Mother Nature/your surroundings and environment. Spend time knowing you are connected with all beings, and also try giving your brain the chance to be somewhere new. Get lost in a new city or park or on a new hike (try not to get *too* lost, and have a charged phone on hand just in case). Give your mind the newness of different surroundings or an experience outside the familiarity of your regular routine. Perhaps take a different route on your way home after school or check out a spot in your community you've never been to before. Name and recognize the land and its Indigenous peoples in which you live, teach, and learn. Before committee, team, or staff meetings, consider reading a land acknowledgment, a statement that recognizes and respects the original Indigenous Inhabitants. Land acknowledgments are simple, powerful ways of showing respect and are steps toward correcting the erasure of the stories and practices of Indigenous people.

Cultivate appreciation for our greater global community and environment.

PRACTICE CELEBRATION

It's really important to model that every child (and adult) has something about them that we can recognize and even celebrate.

—Kristen Ford, Special Education Teacher, New York

VIDEO 8.3

Kristen's strategies apply to both students and educators. She emphasizes the importance of taking time to model kindness and community in her classroom and school environment as a continued practice to model to our students and each other.

https://www.wiley.com/go/happyteacherrevolution

Our brains are wired to respond to rewards. When we celebrate the wins, even the teeny-tiny wins, we are supporting ourselves on the path toward reaching even larger goals. The encouragement here is to practice celebration repeatedly. Continue the practice of celebrating each other instead of just making it a one-time thing.

> According to research by Teresa Amabile from Harvard Business School, "people who tracked their small achievements every day enhanced their motivation. The simple practice of recording your progress helps you to appreciate your small wins which in turn boosts your sense of confidence. Why? Any accomplishment, no matter how small, releases the neurotransmitter dopamine which boosts your mood, motivation and attention. It also signals you to keep doing the activity again and again. What can you celebrate today?" (Rothstein and Stromme, n.d., "Celebrate the Small Stuff," Episode 4.1).

Neuroplastic construction is the ability for the brain to respond to its own activity. As neurons strengthen their communication through their connections of axons and dendrites, these strengthened circuits can activate positive motivation through a dopamine response. As you practice this positive perspective, you are literally rewiring your brain through a positive mindset circuit.

Write a note, text, or email of appreciation, or even just send a meme.

My colleague and I had a pretty sarcastic sense of humor, especially when we were each teaching classes of 39 kindergarteners, which was almost 80 children between the two of us. Making memes and silly jokes was our way not only to get by but also to appreciate and bond with one another. During some of the tough times, we often told each other that if we weren't laughing, we might otherwise be crying. Being able to find something that we could find humor in felt like a lifeline during times I felt like I was drowning. Knowing and naming the gratitude for those folks in my life who are my bright spots also helped me to recognize those pockets of light more and more often.

Code-switch using something tangible to represent or remind you of community.

Put on the T-shirt or wear the swag from the place that represents "community" to you. Be proud and think about yourself as one of something larger than yourself. Wear your community. If you're feeling lonely and isolated, consider showing up in your community even if it may not look or sound the same that it usually does for you. I was feeling an identity crisis while writing this book. I wanted to erase myself and who I am from these pages and not be visible in how this book was birthed into the world. I started spiraling. For me, my feelings were very close to the surface and there was a tenderness in my heart. Instead of skipping the Zoom meeting for my weekly meditation communities, I still showed up but in a way that was aligned for me. I didn't share or contribute verbally with language to the space, yet I still felt like my presence was a contribution because I felt authentically seen. Whether it is showing up for an event even if you're still feeling lonely, or if you are in solitude and craving community, consider wearing a symbol or item that reminds you of your community so that you can remember you are never alone.

APPRECIATE BY LISTENING

> *We have a social justice mission at my school where we have a philanthropic piece to our mission standard, so giving back to the community is a large part of that . . . and it involves a lot of listening. Listen to your students. Listen to your coworkers. Listen to your families. Listening is going to be the biggest thing to make people feel like you care and gives them that sense of belonging that you ultimately want everyone to have and that we want to feel as well.*
>
> —Joey Viola, Charter School Educator, Los Angeles, California

VIDEO 8.4

In the video, Joey describes a practice of being present as a listener, and the importance of our intentional presence as listeners to those around us.

https://www.wiley.com/go/happyteacherrevolution

In a world where we are so dialed in to our digital devices, taking the time to disconnect in order to foster authentic connection is paramount. A *Harvard Business Review* study by Itzchakov and Kluger (2018) illuminates the importance of appreciative listening. The authors' findings suggest that "listening seems to make employees more relaxed, more self-aware of his or her strengths and weaknesses, and more willing to reflect in a non-defensive manner." Appreciative listening can "make employees more likely to cooperate (versus compete) with other colleagues, as they become more interested in sharing their attitudes, but not necessarily in trying to persuade others to adopt them, and more open to considering other points of view."

Consider appreciative listening to be like a muscle; it requires frequent use and practice rather than just a one-and-done singular instance. It requires being present in the moment, putting your phone down, and holding space for someone else with your attention. Make eye contact and try not to get distracted by screens, surroundings, or someone else. Try to resist the urge to interrupt, judge, evaluate, or seek solutions for the speaker.

This practice is incredibly difficult for educators, as we are very much trained to jump in with our "red teacher pen" to circle, underline, and "correct" what we deem as incorrect. Rather, simply be present and attentive without jumping in to try to "fix" any issues at hand. Instead allow for the spaciousness of simply being an attentive listener to the person sharing.

Consider asking thoughtful questions to better understand the perspective of the speaker sharing. Consider asking deeper questions about the topics shared, or simply say "Tell me more." Finally, I invite you not only to listen to the words that the speaker shares but also their nonverbal language. Do they cross their arms or lean back? Maybe they lean toward you during certain points of the conversation. Listening to both verbal and nonverbal cues builds appreciation while simultaneously deepening the human connection between speaker and listener.

Create opportunities or rituals around acts of kindness. This thoughtfulness can be the smallest of gestures, whether it's a compliment on a sticky note, a quick email, or even a brief comment in the hallway. It could be an opportunity to invite students to create thoughtful moments for one another or for other classes. The practice of Thoughtful Thursdays can transcend beyond K–12 education and into higher ed. Auburn University's Office of Inclusion and Diversity is an example of a university incorporating the practice of Thoughtful Thursdays on college campuses. Thoughtful Thursday is an opportunity to be mindful of others, and we hope that the benefits of this practice leak into other days of your week, too!

Practice Thoughtful Thursdays.

I CHOOSE TO
enjoy the
relationships
THAT MATTER
HAPPY TEACHER REVOLUTION

Figure 8.1

9

Supporting Students Who've Experienced Trauma

Teachers and administrators are all caught in the same traps: We are *all* working within a system that is underfunded, given tremendous responsibilities beyond the original scope of our job descriptions, and lack training around adequately supporting fellow humans who've experienced trauma.

The word "trauma" refers to experiencing too much stress, often for too long, and perhaps with not enough support. Chapter 14 shows you how prioritizing your well-being equates to professional development and addresses how to support yourself in grappling with vicarious, or secondhand, trauma.

This chapter identifies strategies around working with individuals who have experienced trauma themselves. You may interact regularly with students, colleagues, caregivers, and/or stakeholders who have direct experience with trauma: previous, current, ongoing, and/or generational.

> Trauma is defined as an adverse experience, violation, or persistent stress in one's life that overwhelms the capacity to cope, typically has long-term emotional, psychological, and physical consequences. Trauma arises from a wide range of experiences and intersecting challenges (which can happen to anyone) that include physical and sexual abuse and violence, caregiver substance abuse and addiction, physical and emotional neglect, loss of a parent, poverty, and, for many, the toxic stress of persistent discrimination and systemic oppression. The essential features of trauma are disempowerment and disconnection from self and others.
>
> —(Education Now News Editor, April 20, 2022)

Trauma can also look very different in terms of how it shows up in your classroom. An educator in Holland describes a student with their hoodie up and head down on the desk; one in the United Kingdom describes a student who desperately tries to people-please and seek approval from adults; an educator in Canada describes a student lashing out by screaming as they run around the room. Each of these instances looks very different, but all of them can be indicators of trauma.

Trauma in a child's life can range from losing a pet or losing a parent, moving neighborhoods or moving countries, experiencing a natural disaster, witnessing an act of gun violence or police brutality, or surviving a global pandemic. There are so many examples of what even counts as trauma (often named "big *T*" or "little *t*" trauma), and they could be issues that people are grappling with on a daily basis. Whether it's surviving a car accident (big *T* trauma) or almost having an accident (little *t* trauma), both instances leave an impression on our lives and are carried in the body.

The study of trauma, or traumatology, is a relatively new field of research; developmental traumatology as a discipline is an even newer frontier. Right now, organizations and systems are just starting to grapple with the effects of trauma and how trauma permeates all aspects of life. Our education system is decades behind what we now know about trauma. Although trauma has become a bit of a buzzword, I hope this section untangles what trauma actually is and how to support those who have experienced it.

"Having a biological system that keeps pumping out stress hormones to deal with real or imagined threats leads to physical problems: sleep disturbances, headaches, unexplained pain, oversensitivity to touch or sound. Being so agitated/shut down prevents the ability to focus attention or to keep concentration" (Van der Kolk, 2015, p. 241). "Being able to feel safe with other people is probably the single most important aspect of mental health; safe connections are fundamental to meaningful and satisfying lives" (p. 128). Numerous studies have demonstrated that social support is the most powerful protection against becoming overwhelmed by stress and trauma; however, social support is not the same as just being in the presence of others (Clark, 2018). "The critical issue is reciprocity: being truly heard and seen by the people around us, feeling that we are held in someone else's mind and heart. For our physiology to calm down, heal and grow we need a visceral feeling of safety" (Van der Kolk, 2015, p. 128).

In summary, we cannot intellectualize our way through healing. The support comes from *doing*—by holding space for yourself to actively listen, by moving the body, by resting in the knowledge that the healing process itself is not linear. While it may be tempting to try to quick-fix our way into expediting a solution, acknowledge that building safe, nurturing relationships where individuals feel truly seen and heard takes time.

STUDY THE SCIENCE OF TRAUMA

Take time to educate yourself on the effects of trauma so that you can respond appropriately and with compassion in the moment to a traumatized individual based on the scientific explanation behind a trauma response. Acknowledge that you are doing the work right this very moment as you read and engage with this chapter. Trauma-informed educational content is something relatively new to the pedagogy and has yet to be formally included in the teaching licensing requirements or credentialing process.

In a trauma response, "the lower brain immediately says *Danger, danger!* and activates the stress-response system, which immediately shuts down the cortex so there's no chance for a reasoned, rational response." In the midst of a trauma response moment, a dysregulated person does not have access to the ability to reason. The more you learn about trauma and stress response, the easier it is to understand certain behaviors you encounter in a workplace, in a relationship, or at school . . . whether it be a rural environment, urban environment, or anywhere in-between" (Perry and Winfrey 2021, p. 224).

> *To be trauma informed, as with other child- and family-serving organizations, schools must be sensitive to the signs of trauma and provide a safe, stable, and understanding environment for students and staff members (Huang et al., 2014). The primary goals are to prevent re-injury or retraumatization by acknowledging trauma and its triggers and to avoid stigmatizing and punishing students (Ford and Courtois, 2013).*
>
> —Krasnoff (2017, p. 6–7)

According to "A Practitioner's Guide to Educating Traumatized Children" by Basha Krasnoff (2017) and recent research, trauma-informed school discipline policies:

- Balance accountability with an understanding of traumatic behavior.
- Teach students school and classroom rules while reinforcing that school is not a violent place and that abusive discipline (which students who have experienced trauma may be accustomed to) is not allowed at school.
- Minimize disruptions to education with an emphasis on positive behavioral supports and behavioral intervention plans.
- Create consistent rules and consequences.
- Model respectful, nonviolent relationships. (p. 7)

> *Build capacity around learning what happens in the brain during a trauma response and what visible behavior is evident.*

Acknowledge that often behaviors are indicative of a trauma response, stay consistent with rules and consequences from a place of calm, and model what respectful interactions with others look like when you interact with both children and adults. Figures 9.1 to 9.4 show what behaviors may be connected to a trauma response.

BEAR WITNESS, OFFER COMPASSION

We all have a deep desire to be seen. Trauma-informed practices requires us to witness the person, their story, and affirm their worthiness for whole and healthy living.

—Mariana Merritt, former Coordinator, Family Engagement, Tennessee

VIDEO 9.1

Mariana shares guidance about responding to trauma.

https://www.wiley.com/go/happyteacherrevolution

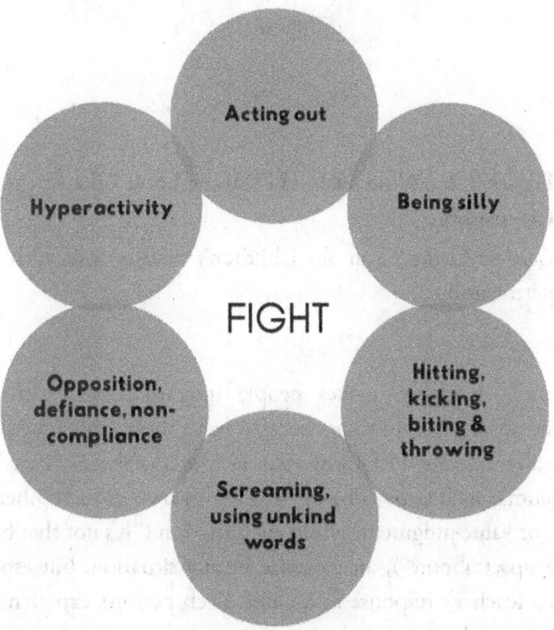

Figure 9.1 What FIGHT Might Look Like in the Classroom.

Concept Credit: Clear Sky Children's Charity, used with permission

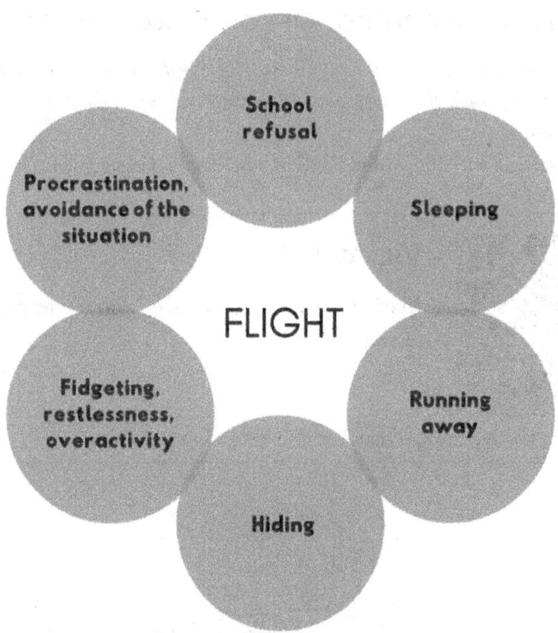

Figure 9.2 What FLIGHT Might Look Like in the Classroom.

Concept Credit: Clear Sky Children's Charity, used with permission

Trauma, understandably, makes people uncomfortable. Unfortunately, that discomfort can lead to responses that leave those who are dealing with trauma feeling unheard and minimized, as Mariana shares. Knee-jerk reactions to trauma, such as by comparing it to our own or to another instance of trauma, or value judgments about the situation ("It's not that bad! What are you so upset about?"), are harmful in any situation, but especially so when it is a teacher's response to a child. Each person's experience is their own and is not to be compared with anyone else's.

Denying or putting a silver lining around someone else's traumatic experience is the brain's way of navigating incredibly painful or uncomfortable situations. To mitigate potential system overloads, people may try to be

Figure 9.3 What FREEZE Might Look Like in the Classroom.

Concept Credit: Clear Sky Children's Charity, used with permission

Press pause. Be present. Listen attentively. Continue developing your own understandings around trauma.

positive for the sake of social desirability (Church, Andreassen, Lorentzen, Melle, and Aas, 2017). But as much as denial or minimization of trauma may put off those uncomfortable feelings, such actions only prolong the inevitable.

As a teacher, I've seen how understanding trauma helps me in planning more engaging lessons and also in helping students understand their emotions so they can better focus on learning. In my classroom, when students are frustrated or disengaged from learning, they can go to the calm-down corner to hug a stuffed toy or meditate, do some deep breathing, read, draw, and play with fidget toys or write in their journals. There are lots of ways to help people regulate their emotions. One day when I was upset, my students told me to decompress in the calm-down corner. It was great. . . . It's easy to see the change when students have what they need. If we keep applying our policies, practices, and budgets toward trauma-informed care, then I think we'll be one step closer to healing.

—Fareeha W., Special Education Teacher, Baltimore, Maryland

When we develop our conscious awareness of trauma, we can model this practice in our classrooms and with our students. It's tempting to try to give

Figure 9.4 What FAWN Might Look Like in the Classroom.

Concept Credit: Clear Sky Children's Charity, used with permission

a silver lining to someone's traumatic share by saying something like "At least ____." While we may intend this kind of message to be supportive, we aren't helping when we attempt to fix anyone or minimize their experiences. Instead, Mariana recommends text like this: "I'm so sorry that happened to you," or "I'm so glad you told me, and I appreciate your vulnerability in sharing." Offering your presence and holding space for a student who may be struggling—without trying to fix anything or heal their hurt—is powerful. When you decide to model practices like listening, deep breathing, or physically processing through movement, be present with yourself and observe any shifts in your own well-being.

FAVOR CONNECTION OVER COMPLIANCE

Now more than ever we must consider self-care completely differently. This is a collective care and collective voice situation. We must have each other's backs.

—Mathew Portell, former Teacher and Principal, Tennessee

VIDEO 9.2

Mathew explains how the tap in/tap out system worked in his school as a trauma-informed practice.

https://www.wiley.com/go/happyteacherrevolution

In the education system, the culture of productivity and the data-driven mindset has embedded within us a tendency to hustle through connection and instead value compliance. But, at the end of the day, it is about cultivating authentic relationships and acknowledging that we are all human beings.

Mathew encourages us to be unapologetic disruptors of systems that are not designed to support students, educators, and families. The best "trauma-informed practices" are ones where you are modeling to your students what social-emotional intelligence looks like in action. Developing a sense of self-awareness means knowing when you need a break. It also includes having the skill set and structures in place to implement the strategy of actually taking a break.

In his video, Mathew describes a strategy his school utilized when he was principal called "tap-in/tap-out." In this school-wide practice, each educator is paired with a fellow staff member whom they can contact when they need a brief break. As Mathew says, "A dysregulated adult cannot regulate a dysregulated child." We have a unique, real-time opportunity to demonstrate a teachable moment to our students about offering ourselves a break. Not only that, but the method also gives us an opportunity to foster meaningful connection in the workplace. Our community only strengthens when we put in place systems that allow us to lean on each other in times of need.

Look at each other in a humanizing way.

Rely on your team or community. Utilize opportunities to tap in or tap out in order to manage your own dysregulated behavior. Creating those structures, such as having a wellness accountability partner or tap-in/tap-out system like Mathew mentioned in the video, require forethought and planning, but consider it a smart return on investment when either you and/or a student are dysregulated. To utilize the tap in/tap out concept, form an alliance with someone else who has a different schedule from your own and reach out to this person in real time to watch your class so you can take a moment for yourself. This person may be a fellow teacher (or two) with a different lunch or planning block, a staff member not responsible for a homeroom class, or others. In my case, my tap in/tap out buddy was my colleague Mr. Turpin. Aware that my schedule often didn't allow for bathroom breaks, Mr. Turpin periodically checked in to ask if I needed to step out. Even if I said no, he encouraged me to take a moment for myself anyway. Having someone ask about my well-being and relieve me when I needed a reprieve was an integral part of incorporating a wellness routine into my workday.

REMEMBER: IT'S NOT ABOUT YOU

It is not my job as an educator to fix behaviors but instead to support families and children.

—Keeli, School Librarian, Tennessee

VIDEO 9.3

Keeli talks about her own growth as an educator and about the value of not taking things personally in the classroom.

https://www.wiley.com/go/happyteacherrevolution

When a child disrupts your carefully planned lesson, raises their voice in anger, or refuses to abide by class norms, you may read their behavior as a response or reaction specifically to you personally. In reality, the child may be showing behavior that stems from trauma. As many as half of children in public schools have had three or more adverse childhood experiences (ACEs), which means that a great many children are coming to school carrying the weight of trauma (Perry and Winfrey, 2021, p. 223). When we take student behaviors personally, we're missing an opportunity to support our students who have experienced trauma. Even worse, our reactions can shame students or inflame situations.

What we experience in the present moment is filtered by the lower parts of our brain before getting to the cortex. All incoming sensory information from the present moment is compared to and influenced by the memories of previous experiences, and is first processed in the lower, more reactive areas of the brain before reaching the rational, "thinking" areas. (Perry and Winfrey, 2021, p. 223)

If you can take a moment to remember the neuroscience behind a trauma response and also give a dysregulated person time to process after the incident, they will be able to access the rational or thinking area of the brain.

QTIP: Quit Taking It Personally!

When you are able to detach with kindness, you are better able to support a person who is dysregulated. As Keeli mentions in her video, taking a trauma response personally will ultimately lead to you becoming dysregulated—and then there's twice as many dysregulated people as there were to begin with! Give yourself permission to take a time out and reconnect once everyone has had an opportunity to regain their calm. In the classroom, you may institute a specific routine or procedure around quiet time or self-reflection time. Perhaps you use a symbolic cue (a physical item that you put on your desk or don), and students know not to talk to you when it is visible. Or it could be a practice you institute with your students, such as everyone quietly journals together or works independently so that you have time to deescalate or not engage with students.

If a repair is needed, co-create a plan with your student(s) around what to do differently next time. This co-creation is an opportunity for both parties to empathize, better understand one another, and feel like active participants in identifying helpful solutions going forward.

PRACTICE RESPONDING WITHOUT HARMING

Trauma can impact our genes, white blood cells, heart, gut, lungs, and brain, our thinking, feeling, behaving, parenting, teaching, coaching, consuming, creating, prescribing, arresting, sentencing. . . . So, depending upon your perspective—your worldview—and your own history of trauma and loss, you will have some unique version of trauma-informed.

v—*Perry and Winfrey, What Happened to You? (2021, p. 219)*

VIDEO 9.4

In the video, Mathew Portell, former Principal and current Founder of the Trauma Informed Educators Network Podcast, shares how an educator's response itself could be traumatic.

https://www.wiley.com/go/happyteacherrevolution

In his video, Mathew acknowledges that he likely inflicted some trauma on students simply by employing physical restraint and containment strategies—and suspension—that he had been trained to enact in response to certain behaviors. Now he advocates inviting students into the experience, creating a conversation rather than talking "at" them in a one-sided dynamic.

Unfortunately, as I have mentioned, the education system is slow to change. Not only that, but the education system itself has been a source of trauma for those operating within it. We cannot be trauma informed until we examine the built-in biases within current pedagogy and also in ourselves. Bruce D. Perry, child psychologist and neuroscientist, believes that

> if you don't recognize the built-in biases in yourself and the structural biases in your systems—biases regarding race, gender, sexual orientation—you can't truly be trauma-informed. Marginalized peoples—excluded, minimized, shamed—are traumatized peoples, because humans are fundamentally relational creatures. To be excluded or dehumanized in an organization, community, or society you are part of results in prolonged, uncontrollable stress that is sensitizing. Marginalization is a fundamental trauma. (Perry and Winfrey, 2021, p. 220)

Dr. Perry shares that the long-term effects of stress are determined by the pattern of stress activation. When the stress-response systems are activated in unpredictable, extreme, or prolonged ways, the systems become overactive and overly reactive and thus sensitized. Over time, this can lead to functional vulnerability. Since the stress-response systems collectively reach all parts of the brain and body, this response places emotional, social, mental, and physical health at risk. In contrast, predictable, moderate, and controllable activation of the stress-response systems, such as developmentally appropriately challenges in education, sport, and music, can lead to stronger, more flexible stress-response capability—in other words, to resilience (Perry and Winfrey, 2021).

Acknowledge the gaps in pedagogy around trauma-informed practices.

Paul C. Gorski, founder of the Equity Literacy Institute and EdChange, shares that "school-wide change has to begin with individuals. It might start with two teachers finding each other" (2019). While we continue the collective fight

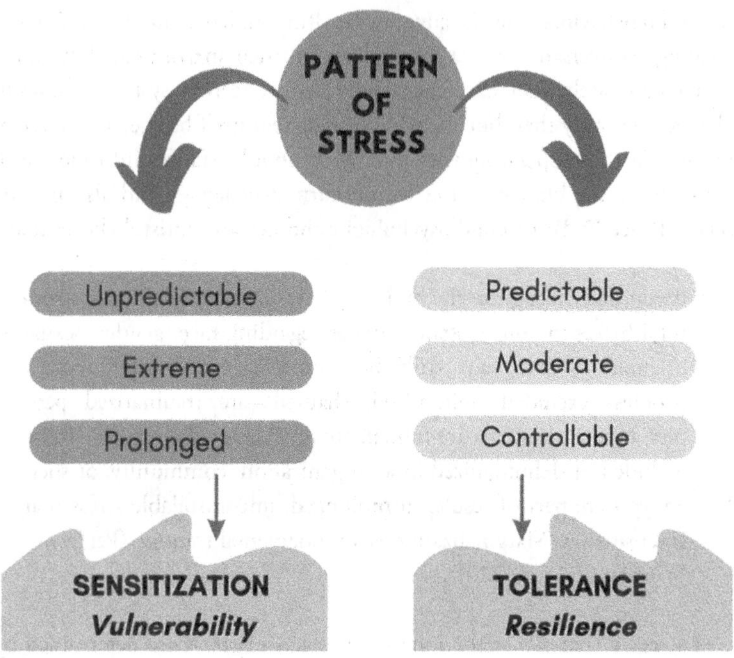

Figure 9.5 Patterns of Stress Activation.
Source: Perry and Winfrey (2021, p. 57). Printed with permission.

to eliminate global injustices, we can trust in the foundation we are actively creating to be more trauma informed.

Practice self-awareness and release any attachment to previous or current educational pedagogy that may not be grounded in a trauma-informed or trauma-researched response. Acknowledge and be accountable for what you may have perpetuated or not questioned. Then, without guilt, shame, or judgment, make the conscious decision to do better. We are each constantly evolving and growing, so take time to acknowledge your own personal growth in this journey. Consider what body awareness looks like for you as you are sitting with these emotions. Invite your students to be present in their own bodies, as well. Often we do not have the time or space for meaningful integration, so consider embedding just a few minutes or create a brief routine around body check-in during the course of your day for yourself and for your students. Rather than attempting to restrain, minimize, or discredit students in any way, consider taking a moment to practice nervous system regulation by being present in the body. This practice not only supports your own well-being, but it also is an opportunity to model this self-awareness to those around you like your students, colleagues, and other stakeholders.

Personal Growth

10

Engaging in Self-Care with Students 2

Create a Playlist Together

The idea of creating a music playlist together is inspired by my experiences presenting at the Hip Hop Ed Conference in New York City in 2019. This incredible gathering, led by Professor Christopher Emdin at Columbia's Teachers College, changed me professionally and is totally different from any conference I have had the chance to be a part of and share my research within.

The idea is to cipher a playlist together. Perhaps the playlist is seasonal, or when a new chapter/unit begins, or at other relevant times. Although you can develop the playlist with your team and colleagues, also consider what it could look like when created with your classroom community. Choose songs without profanity or vulgar lyrics that are school appropriate yet still representative of your classroom. Perhaps have each student contribute a song recommendation and contribute your own favorite tunes, too.

REGULATE BY EMBODYING

VIDEO 10.1

In this video, Taylor Gonzalez explains how to embody feelings instead of intellectualizing your way through them.

https://www.wiley.com/go/happyteacherrevolution

Name the feelings as they are happening in the body, and/or consciously embody those emotions as Taylor describes in Video 10.1. Name the physical experiences in the body to model to students what this practice could look like. Does the body respond with a quickening of the heart, shallower breathing, tension in the shoulders? Practice naming what is happening in the body alongside students to allow you both to better understand how trauma appears. Giving voice to this experience lessens the charge and power trauma has over us and also allows us to drop back into the body by being present within ourselves rather than numbing out.

SHARE A MEAL TOGETHER

One of my favorite things was to invite my students and their families to contribute to a cultural day focusing on the cuisines of different cultures represented in our classroom. Not only was it a way to foster authentic connection and build relationships with families and stakeholders, but it also was an opportunity to bond over a meal together with my students. Be sure to be mindful of allergies and dietary restrictions, but also encourage students to try new foods and enjoy the opportunity to get to know one another in a relaxed atmosphere.

REST AND DIGEST

Some parts of the school day have intense levels of stimulation, whether this is a chaotic cafeteria, noisy hallways during transitions between bell rings, or spontaneous fire drills. I realized that my students and I both craved the chance to de-escalate by sitting quietly as a community in the classroom. In my classroom, the "rest and digest" period occurred in my classroom after lunch in the cafeteria. We transitioned into the classroom and took a few breaths (or a few minutes) to sit quietly. Our culture is not designed to digest big heavy moments or big heavy meals. In your professional role as a leader, consider creating opportunities for collective rest and perhaps ask students to take three deep breaths together. In opportunities to witness a sunset, the moon, or a beautiful flower blossoming, it is wise to take in the moment, rest in the moment, digest the moment, and be present in the moment rather than rushing to the next thing. Not only is "rest and digest" a practice in being present within oneself on an individual level, but holding space within the collective community to cultivate stillness amplifies the power of the practice.

11

Establishing Boundaries 2

Specify Your Limits

Video 11.1

Heather shares authentic advice around setting boundaries with relationships.

https://www.wiley.com/go/happyteacherrevolution

It's okay if your work colleagues are not your family. It's okay if you don't feel comfortable drinking with your colleagues at the bar for a happy hour. It's okay to be part of the community as long as it looks the way you feel comfortable. One of my favorite ways to frame a boundary is by considering the context of what aligns for me and specifying those terms: "As long as it looks like this _______." I realized that I felt uncomfortable drinking with colleagues because of past experiences that quickly devolved into unprofessional situations. I didn't mind spending time with colleagues outside of the workplace, but I realized that there were certain types of boundaries that felt safe for me. I realized that this was an invitation to frame a boundary that fostered connection in a way that felt true and authentic to me.

Choose Boundaries over Burnout

Licensed therapist Nedra Glover Tawwab shares her experience working with patients in her practice:

> Many of the clients I see in my practice report issues with work-life balance. For fourteen years, I've observed people doing the work of two people, not leaving work on time, working after hours (evenings and weekends), not using allocated personal days, and volunteering for projects they don't have time to do. They do this all in the nature of being a "good employee." I have cautioned them, "The more you appear to handle, the more work you'll be expected to handle." (2021, pp. 224–225)

Give yourself permission to set boundaries in the workplace and with colleagues. Just because you're at work doesn't mean you are not allowed to set limits. If you do not articulate your own needs and boundaries, resentment could build toward your colleagues, your boss, and maybe even the profession as a whole.

Express Yourself

Leaning on someone is a way to foster community and mutual understanding. It can be incredibly uncomfortable and challenging to find the right words, and that's okay, too.

Practice saying these sentence starters rather than suppressing or self-silencing your voice and your experience:

- "I won't be able to take on any additional projects."
- "I need more assistance with my workload."

- "Thank you for inviting me to hang out this weekend, but I won't be able to make it." (Taawwab. 2021, p. 227)
- "This doesn't align for me at the moment."
- "I can't commit to this now."
- "I need to wait and see."

BE GENTLE WITH YOURSELF

Be gentle with yourself, as true "community" may feel like an unfamiliar experience if you haven't felt it before. Belonging within a community may feel unfamiliar at first, especially within a newly found or evolving connection with individuals who align with you. This feeling of unfamiliarity might even seem like a lack of safety or cause you to become hypervigilant. I didn't realize how uncomfortable a true sense of community and connection could feel until I found it for the first time, when I felt like I could truly be my most authentic self. The image I was picturing was the way a mattress unfolds for the first time. Some kinks need to be worked out and some time is needed for it to completely unfurl. This integration process is so important and necessary; it is also something to consider when being with the individuals within your community who may also be experiencing this type of collective care for the very first time.

PART IV

Reflecting/ Integrating 2

Naming Your Support

Write 3 people in the blanks below that you can go to who are your cheerleaders, rooting for you, and you can count on to gas you up. Bookmark this page when you may feel a sense of isolation or are craving connection and reach out to one (or all!) of the following individuals:

1. ____________________
2. ____________________
3. ____________________

GUIDED MEDITATION: CULTIVATING JOY AND CONNECTION WITH OTHERS

By Elayne Mendoza

VIDEO P4.1

Elayne narrates a guided meditation with written text included below for you to consider deepening your connection with others.

https://www.wiley.com/go/happyteacherrevolution

Take this opportunity to pause and enter the present moment wherever you are right now. Whether that is at your desk, inside of your car, or in the comfort of your home, start to feel the surface beneath you, lengthen your spine, and now relax your shoulders.

And now gently close your eyes, sensing your body and observing how you are feeling right now. And without creating any attachments to what you are noticing just simply feel.

Notice what is present and what is really coming forward inside of your body.

And now let's move your awareness to your breath.

You can begin by slowly inhaling through your nose and exhale through your nose

Deep breath in.

And deep breath out.

Inhale.

Exhale.

Into your nose and out through your mouth.

Two more, deep breath in through your nose, and exhale audible sigh through your mouth.

Deep breath in through your nose and exhale an audible sigh through your mouth.

And as you continue to breathe, move your awareness to your heart space and feel the sensations that are present.

And I want you to picture your heart as a blossoming yellow rose. A yellow rose represents joy and friendship. It evokes feelings of warmth, love, care, and hope.

And now visualize your heart as a yellow rose holding this meeting.

Consider the people who bring you happiness, or present any challenges as well. Either/or can be welcomed into this meditation.

Connect to your heart once more, and visualize, sending love and joy to everyone you come in contact with.

Breathe in warmth

and exhale joy.

Breathe in warmth

and exhale joy.

Breathe in warmth

and exhale joy.

And in your mind's eye say, I value myself as I value you.

And may we both experience happiness, and joy.

May we all have the capacity to feel the tender love and care that we all yearn for.

And may you share and receive this energy to those you are surrounded by.

Inhale through your nose.

And exhale, sigh it out.

And now pause.

Opening your eyes slowly, and bringing gentle movement into your toes and fingers.

Returning back to reality and lead with love.

SOMATIC EMBODIMENT EXPERIENCE

VIDEO P4.2

Maya Basik, former educator and embodiment teacher, guides us through an opportunity to be present in the physical body in an embodiment practice to support you in cultivating joy with others; and experiencing relationships from a sovereign, well-resourced, and deeply rooted-in-self place.

https://www.wiley.com/go/happyteacherrevolution

BREATHING EXPERIENCE

VIDEO P4.3

"Breathing matters to me more than any of the individual poses, and, since I've started practicing, I've become much more aware of the constant presence of breath as well as the importance of breath as well as the power of breath," says Keith Golden, Musician and Movement Teacher, who guides us through a calming breathing experience in this video.

https://www.wiley.com/go/happyteacherrevolution

SCENT EXPERIENCE

Safety note: Many essential oils are toxic to pets, and please do not ingest any essential oils.

Suggested scent example for deepening connection with others: *Lavender (Lavandul Angustifolia)*

SOUNDTRACK EXPERIENCE

Additional music suggestions are available for your listening enjoyment on the official Happy Teacher Revolution Playlist on Spotify.

"A Change Is Gonna Come" by Sam Cooke

"Find My Own Way" by GRiZ, Wiz Khalifa

"Volunteers" by Jefferson Airplane

"Lean on Me" by Bill Withers

TASTE EXPERIENCE

This recipe is perfect for lunch or dinner, hot or cold. I like to add a touch of cayenne pepper because I'm a big fan of heat, but it's totally optional. Also consider adding some of your favorite toppings or add-ins like cherry tomatoes, cucumbers, green onions, whatever!

CURRY QUINOA

2 tablespoons olive oil
1 medium onion, chopped
½ tablespoon curry powder
¼ teaspoon cayenne pepper (optional)
1 cup quinoa (all red or a mix of red, white, and black)
¼ teaspoon salt
Pinch of pepper
1¼ cups vegetable stock (or water)

Heat the olive oil in a heavy medium saucepan until shimmering. Add the chopped onions and sauté until translucent. Add curry powder and optional cayenne. Toast for 30 seconds as it becomes fragrant.

Add quinoa, stirring to coat grains with oil and spices. Season with salt and pepper to taste, adding more curry powder if you prefer a stronger flavor.

Add vegetable stock (or water) and combine all ingredients. Bring to a boil, covered. Reduce heat to low and simmer, covered, until water is absorbed and quinoa is tender, about 20 minutes. Try not to peek!

Remove pan from the heat and let stand, covered, for 5 minutes. Fluff with a fork and keep covered to keep warm. Leftovers are great to reheat or even served cold.

I like to have this as lunch the next day and will reheat in the microwave in the teachers' lounge . . . or if the microwave is nasty (real talk) or not available, I enjoy this cold and add toppings like chopped scallions, sliced almonds, diced cucumbers, fresh dill, you name it! Customize this and use the general quinoa recipe as your base to get creative!

POETRY EXPERIENCE

Community

When I think of
the people
who are lifting me up
I can feel them
Hear them
See them
I wonder if they
will ever understand
That
they
healed me
That
they
saved me
And here I thought
I was teaching them
Community matters
and *nothing*
else
does

—Christina Costa, from *Kiss Your Brain: Diagnosis Diaries* (2021, p. 53). Printed with permission.

I CHOOSE WHAT
to do next time and
what to
STOP DOING
HAPPY TEACHER REVOLUTION

Figure P4.1

PART V

Advocating for Yourself and for Systemic Change

What is really valuable and important about Happy Teacher Revolution is that it's not just an independent journey, but we are thinking about systemic change within our organizations. We are thinking about how we can be vulnerable with our colleagues in healthy ways that enable us to provide community care together and to support each other together. Because, unless we acknowledge the important role of emotions as part of organizational culture and not just as a private experience, we're not going to change things for teachers.

—Kristabel Stark, Researcher and Educator, University of Vermont

VIDEO P5.1

Kristabel Stark, researcher and coauthor of "A Vision for Teachers' Emotional Well-Being," describes the importance of advocating for yourself and movements like Happy Teacher Revolution in order to enact systemic change.

https://www.wiley.com/go/happyteacherrevolution

I started the Happy Teacher Revolution Movement because I was inspired by the consciousness-raising groups of the Civil Rights Movement and the Women's Liberation Movement. I was inspired to create collective change at the grassroots level by creating a simple resource, tool, and platform to amplify voices that have been historically silenced. I felt called to create a framework to support educators by inviting individuals who have not been invited to have a seat at the table to share their voices and stories.

Happy Teacher Revolution is a movement and absolutely a revolution in every sense of the word. This movement was designed to disrupt the status quo. I recognize this statement is a bold one to make, not just as an educator but also as a woman. While I may be the founder of this movement, I am simply the messenger through which this vision has come to life. The greater collective of individual educators who similarly align around prioritizing the mental health and well-being of ourselves, each other, and of course our students is the driving force behind moving the needle toward collective change.

In order to understand each other, we have to understand the histories and lenses through which we see one another. Emotion is a universal language, and as we cultivate our own social emotional competence, we deepen our vocabulary of emotion not only to better connect within ourselves but also to connect with each other.

As we share more of our authentic selves and our own stories with others, we are able to be heard and seen. But even further, by living and speaking with integrity about ourselves, we are able to model to others by making visible what these social-emotional learning competencies actually look like, sound like, and feel like in action.

The systemic change component of education is absolutely necessary, especially as we consider the history of social injustice and inequality perpetuated by the education system itself. And we have to prioritize our own sustainability within this important work so as to avoid burnout and fatigue, which could potentially be so deeply experienced that we aren't able to continue the fight for justice and enact change.

> I think part of unlearning these vast and failing systems is to learn to trust ourselves and our own wisdom, but we must also challenge the status quo and unpack how we play into domination. Holding ourselves accountable and listening to our morality and our gut is key, but then we must act. (Róisín, 2022, p. 77)

We can have faith in our own ability to be autonomous while simultaneously cultivating the self-awareness necessary to recognize our own areas of growth. We can hold the duality of both trusting ourselves while recognizing that we are going to engage in an ongoing practice of unpacking. The action component does not need to be monumental; rather, it requires a consideration of the importance of even "small" actions in the name of systemic change.

In her book *The Lifelong Activist: How to Change the World Without Losing Your Way* (2006), Hilary Rettig shares:

> Burnout is the act of involuntarily leaving activism, or reducing one's level of activism. . . When an activist burns out, she typically derails her career and damages her self-esteem and relationships. She also deprives her organization and movement of her valuable experience and wisdom. The worst problem, however, may be that when an activist burns out she deprives younger activists of a mentor, thus making them more likely to burn out. (p. 16)

In your work to enact systemic change, it is absolutely necessary that you continue to loop back to the first section of this text to consider prioritizing the well-being of the most important individual: YOU.

It doesn't help anyone if you resist who you are and what you need. True social innovation is born from a place of empowerment rather than self-censorship or fear. When we are not honest with ourselves, we are more prone to burnout. As Rettig writes: "The only cure for this kind of burnout is to be truthful about who you are, what your values are and what your needs are, and to start reorganizing your life around that truth" (p. 18). Living in alignment with your own core beliefs will be the foundation that you can trust and root down into when the storms try to wear you down throughout this roadtrip you're on to claim joy.

> School leaders set the vision for their schools, and having a shared vision is crucial to success. Leaders can start to reform their school cultures by simply acknowledging the difficult emotional work that teachers engage in every day and sending a clear message that experiencing a wide range of emotions is not a reflection of personal weakness. More concretely, leaders can provide educators with opportunities, such as HTR support groups, to give and receive social support.
>
> Creating school cultures that support teachers' emotional well-being is challenging but necessary. As one educator explained to us, "The real work is to be well." To thrive, teachers require organizational policies, norms, and leadership that affirm the complex emotional demands of their jobs. . . ; the wide range of emotions that they naturally experience . . .; and the work that it takes to regulate their outward emotional expressions.
>
> —(Stark, Daulat, and King, 2022, p. 29)

12

Letting Yourself Be Autonomous

We can choose to engage in a revolution to change the organizational dynamics of our schools so that teachers' well-being is prioritized.

—Stark, Daulat, and King, A Vision for Teachers' Emotional Well-Being (2022, p. 30)

The desire for more autonomy was one of the single most common themes that came up in my research around supporting teacher well-being and reducing burnout. Autonomy is also one of the core tenets of Carol Ryff's Psychological Scale of Well-Being (Ryff and Keyes, 1995), and for good reason. It is absolutely essential for us to feel agency and freedom over ourselves and our own lives.

In the depths of my most stressful years in the classroom, I often found myself waking up to a recurring dream as my alarm clock buzzed. The dream was always the same. It started with me sitting in the backseat of a car. The

Autonomy

car would be careening down the highway, and I would suddenly realize that no one was in the driver's seat. The dream continues with me attempting to clamber from the backseat into the front to get behind the wheel and pump the brakes. The dream ends with me barely making it into the front seat and careening into the abyss like the last level of Rainbow Road in *Mario Kart*. Why mention this? I felt like my life was out of control and I wasn't even the one behind the wheel to steer it back in the right direction. I realized I had the chance to deepen my well-being by developing my own trust in myself. It is a gargantuan act to notice your own needs and be able to name what you *truly* want. It is a completely second and separate gesture and skill set to then act on those deeply felt desires and intuition.

I realized that so much of what I was doing as "Miss Thomas" was a performance. I was performing what I believed was what society deemed as a "good teacher" without actually being true to my authentic self as "Danna." I wondered: How do I perform "good teacher"? Someone give me a lesson plan, a manual, or a handbook on how to be the epitome of an ideal teacher. (In my mind it was Miss Honey from *Matilda*, but her ease and well-rested demeanor couldn't feel further from my current reality.) Eventually, I learned how to perform this role of "good teacher," but it was at the expense of the spirit within me.

Your core identity is who you are. Right now I want to affirm that you are a powerful human being and that you have a profound impact. There are teachers out there who are so busy performing a role that they lose the core of who they are. The more you perform the role and the more you construct a system for the sake of someone else liking you or approving of you, not only are you performing this identity but you are simultaneously avoiding your core identity. In addition, we are modeling this to children who are human beings actively developing their own social-emotional intelligence.

When you walk into a school that doesn't teach to your soul but only teaches to your mind, you lose an aspect of humanity. Thus, you are responding to the fact that the role is more important than core identity, which puts you in a position of systemic oppression. In other words, you are existing within a system of violence oppressing your core identity. The human condition of our caregivers is being erased, and we must bring light to the human condition of the collective. Teachers are human beings, not human doings, and the impact of denying our own personhood across all dimensions of mental and behavioral health for our caregivers and those that they care for is an assault to humanity.

BE A PIONEER

Avoid people who are unhappy and disgruntled about the possibilities for transforming education. They are the enemy of the spirit of the teacher.

—Christopher Emdin, *For White Folks Who Teach in the Hood* (2016, p. 208)

VIDEO 12.1

Donna Fernandez from Houston Independent School District shares her excitement for pioneering the first Happy Teacher Revolution large-scale pilot cohort in the state of Texas and the implications of supporting systemic change around well-being at the district level from a leadership perspective.

https://www.wiley.com/go/happyteacherrevolution

You have a choice to make an autonomous act, no matter how seemingly small, with the intention to enact systemic change. That single gesture in and of itself is a radical step in the right direction. As a collective movement to prioritize the mental health and well-being of all humans within a system that was not designed with our well-being in mind, we also must collectively organize to make meaningful disruption. The most powerful way to harness your power as a pioneer is to be scientific about your efforts.

When I first started Happy Teacher Revolution, I wanted to measure the impact of its implementation as intentionally as possible. This initially led to me utilizing the Maslach Burnout Inventory (Maslach, Jackson, and Leiter, 1996), but my perspective completely shifted when our world experienced a global pandemic and I deepened my understanding of positive psychology research. Instead of operating from a deficit mindset in measuring burnout, I wanted instead to clarify well-being principles from a scientific perspective so that wellness seemed less shrouded in mystery.

The next step in creating systemic change around supporting the well-being of caregivers and education professionals was to collect data that was statistically significant. While I am so grateful for the pioneering Revolutionaries who have been trailblazers in launching Happy Teacher Revolution meetings, the next step in deepening lasting impact is measuring the effects of *entire* schools and/or districts adopting Happy Teacher Revolution programming. In order to scale and sustain results, pilot sites not only enroll Revolutionaries but also launch train-the-trainer professional development to support entire cohorts of change-makers long term.

Once entire schools and school districts decided to pilot the Happy Teacher Revolution program and meetings, we were able to collect meaningful data, which shaped our first published research: "A Vision for Teachers' Emotional Well-Being."

> Self-care is not enough to help teachers manage their stress. Organizational change is needed. The COVID-19 pandemic has forced education stakeholders to grapple with fundamental questions about the role of schools in our society. As a result, many educators have found creative new ways to provide not just academic instruction but also emotional care, ensuring that their students are safe and well in a tumultuous time. But these efforts have not come without a cost. For many teachers, adjusting to virtual and hybrid education was highly stressful, and that stress was only compounded by the worldwide pandemic-related confusion across all areas of society. And so an already stressful job was made even more difficult. For many teachers, the return to in-person schooling hasn't improved matters, as they've had to support students who are having difficulty adjusting to being back in the classroom, even as they face intense political scrutiny regarding the nature and content of their curriculum.
>
> In this season of reimagining the purpose and meaning of schools, many educational stakeholders are crafting new visions of how schools can support all children. . . . We encourage them to go a step further to ask, *What is our vision for teachers' emotional well-being?* We challenge educational stakeholders to imagine what it would look like for teachers not just to survive, but to *thrive* in their jobs—and to consider what needs to change at the organizational level to make this possible. (Stark, Daulat, and King, 2022, pp. 24–25)

Advocate for a Happy Teacher Revolution pilot site.

As I continue to lead and listen to our Revolutionaries who facilitate meetings, I recognize that this is a radical movement because there have not been multitiered systems of support targeting the well-being of the adults within the education system. To be a pioneer within this movement, consider getting trained yourself and advocating for the long-term implementation of the program that is sustainable not only for you but also for your community. We must consider systemic change as synonymous with sustainable change by scaling impact through multiple touch points and multiple staff members completing professional development training as cohorts of Revolutionaries. At the organizational level, we must consider investing in statistically significant research and evidence-based initiatives like Happy Teacher Revolution as long-term interventions to support the mental health and well-being of adults and students. To find out more about training opportunities and how to advocate for becoming a Happy Teacher Revolution pilot site, check out www.HappyTeacherRevolution.com.

MAKE THE INVISIBLE VISIBLE

Whether it's at school board meetings or people at dinner parties that say you have summers off I realized I can be an advocate and educate them.

—Jackie Vance, Central Oregon Community College Faculty Member Bend, Oregon

VIDEO 12.2

Benita Moyers, recipient of the National Education Association's award for Teaching Excellence, describes the impact of the Happy Teacher Revolution movement in her life, specifically being mindful of well-being and taking action to bring about visibility and awareness.

https://www.wiley.com/go/happyteacherrevolution

Part of systemic change is bringing to light that which has gone unnamed, uncompensated, and unacknowledged.

> Moral injury . . . , originally discussed in relationship to transgressing moral beliefs and values during wartime among military personnel, has expanded beyond this context to include similar emotions experienced by healthcare professionals, first responders, and others experiencing moral emotions resulting from actions taken or observations made during traumatic events or circumstances. (Koenig and Al Zaben, 2021, p. 2989)

The work occurs when we can name and acknowledge the importance and load of task shifting as well as the invisible weight of all of the responsibilities and asks that teachers face day in and day out.

Name and give voice to the moral injury you've experienced.

Compared to burnout, which implies that providers feel overwhelmed because of their position, moral injury shifts the focus. It is not just the fact of being a caregiver: The system and culture are the issues (Kirsch, n.d. [2021]). It would be an oversight if I didn't mention evaluating moral injury in the context of COVID-19 and a global pandemic. The important part of systemic change is being able to amplify your own voice and perspective within a container that affirms your experience. In Happy Teacher Revolution, we call this container the Happy Teacher Revolution meeting. The meeting is the time and space where participants can feel, deal, and be real about the social-emotional and intellectual demands that they face on the job.

Lean on your union.

When Happy Teacher Revolution first began, a statewide union supported their educators by enrolling union leaders into our program to become certified Revolutionaries. This offered union leaders an opportunity to foster community in their own regions while also deepening connections between the leaders themselves as they stepped into this new facilitation role.

If you are a member of a union or have access to union support, use it. That's what unions are there for. You don't need to reinvent the wheel and can self-advocate to get help. Speak up. Know that your union cannot read your mind, and also know that unions exist to be in your corner. You may be grappling with things and issues that you need to bring visibility to in order to make change. When you make the invisible visible to your union, you are integrating systemic change through a support system that already exists.

ADVOCATE FOR ACCESSIBILITY AND EQUALITY

When you know better, do better.

—Maya Angelou

Being autonomous means raising your personal consciousness and awareness to stand for what you know is right even if it's not specifically asked of or directed at you. Claiming your personal sovereignty is also an incredible opportunity to interrupt the old pattern and enact systemic change.

There may be folks who do not even realize they are perpetuating limited beliefs and excluding others. Part of being autonomous is creating opportunities to be more inclusive of the individuals you are surrounded by, even if you're the first one to take the conscientious steps to do so. Actively advocate for fellow staff, students, and stakeholders when it comes to accessibility and equality for all.

Consider actively inclusive alternatives inspired by the work and advocacy of Justin Graves of HESONWHEELS, to specifically put a person before their abilities. Some examples include saying: "upcoming activities" instead of "next steps", "as you may observe" instead of "as you can see", or "I support you" instead of "I stand with you".

Distinguish calling in from calling out.

When addressing systemic change, it can be beneficial to consider how you are mindfully communicating to others. Tiffany Jewell explains the topic in *This Book Is Anti-Racist: 20 Lessons on How to Wake Up, Take Action, and Do the Work*:

> If you call someone in, you circle back to a hurtful or oppressive comment they made in private. If you call someone out, you let them know their comment was hurtful in a public space. . . .

> Over the years I've learned that a lot of folx [*sic*] prefer to call others in and to be called in themselves, after someone says or does something that is harmful to an oppressed group. . . .
>
> To call someone in, you can also email or message them and explain why and how what they said is hurtful. . . .
>
> Calling someone in can be a pretty effective way of working with someone to change their problematic behavior. They're more likely to hear what you are saying if it feels like a more gentle approach. It does require you to be compassionate and invest some of your time and energy. . . .
>
> Calling someone out can also be effective. It does require you to take a risk. You will be bringing attention to someone's oppressive and detrimental behavior. It allows for others to hear you and creates greater accountability as there's more than one person involved.
>
> We will all have moments when we are the folx [*sic*] on the receiving end of a call-in or call-out. If you are the person who has just been called out, instead of bristling in defense, or getting upset, think about what the other person has just said. Hear them. Thank them for their comment and acknowledge you listened. Use that as a moment to teach yourself, open up dialogue, and dig deeper. This is how we all learn and move forward. (2020, pp. 112–114)

Know that when you try this for the first time, it may be clunky, unpolished, and imperfect. It may also feel incredibly uncomfortable and unfamiliar. You may even second-guess yourself and question if you should've even called them in or called them out in the first place. You may make mistakes and be completely imperfect, but know that every action you take is also an incredible opportunity to learn and grow. Know that I believe in you and am rooting for you!

You Can't Spell "Resist" Without "Rest"

> *The idea of resistance is central to the message of rest and to our life as human beings. . . . Rest is soul care because rest deliberately pays close attention to the deepest parts of you. Rest places soul care at the center*

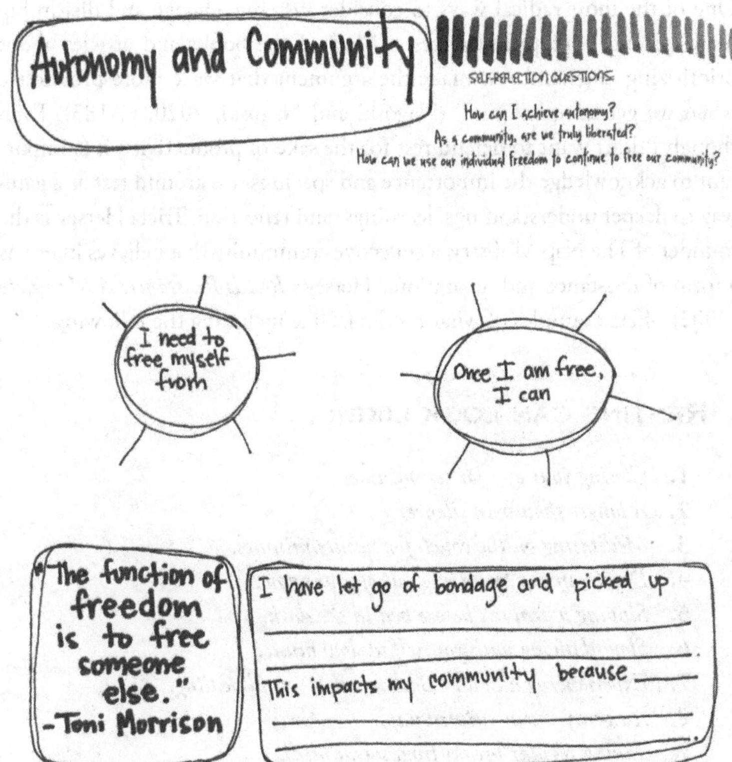

Figure 12.1 ***Soundless Cries Don't Lead to Healing,*** **Valencia D. Clay, 2016.**

Reprinted with permission of Valencia D. Clay.

> *of our wellness and liberation. None of us will get free without resisting toxic systems that blind us to the truth of who and what we are. We should be curious about our souls and the ways rest can comfort, heal, and uncover what grind culture has never allowed us to feel. Our bodies have information to share with us.*
>
> —Tricia Hersey, *Rest Is Resistance: A Manifesto* (2022, p. 129)

One of the most radical ways to consider systemic change and disrupting toxic systems is to prioritize rest. "Most of the books and articles about prioritizing sleep and rest make the argument that we're more productive when we get adequate rest" (Nagoski and Nagoski, 2020, p. 183). Even though I don't want to defend rest for the sake of productivity, it is important to acknowledge the importance and spaciousness around rest as a gateway to deeper understandings, learnings, and reflection. Tricia Hersey is the founder of The Nap Ministry, a collective community that believes in rest as a form of resistance and reparations. Hersey's *Rest Is Resistance: A Manifesto* (2002) offers examples of what rest looks like including the following.

RESTING CAN LOOK LIKE . . .

1. *Closing your eyes for ten minutes.*
2. *A longer shower in silence.*
3. *Meditating on the couch for twenty minutes.*
4. *Daydreaming by staring out of a window.*
5. *Sipping warm tea before bed in the dark.*
6. *Slow-dancing with yourself to slow music.*
7. *Experiencing a Sound Bath or other sound healing.*
8. *A twenty-minute timed nap.*
9. *Taking regular breaks from social media.*
10. *Not immediately responding to texts and emails.*
11. *Deep listening to a full music album.*

—Tricia Hersey, *Rest Is Resistance: A Manifesto* (2022, p. 85)

Start resting.

Resting doesn't need to be an entire day devoted to rest. It can be something that starts small with just a moment, a breath, a minute to rest. It also isn't a singular limited definition. Rest can look and feel different based on your body's unique needs at the time.

Consider intentionally doing nothing rather than reaching for your phone. Take a moment to be present with your body, even as you are reading these words, and do something in this moment to offer yourself rest. The purpose of being present with oneself is not for work's sake but to disrupt the patriarchal, capitalistic, and White supremacy grind culture that prioritizes productivity over humanity.

GIVE YOURSELF FILLER EPISODE DAYS

> *We all need time to sit back and let someone else be the main character—even if it goes against our productivity-powered culture. People feel guilty doing nothing or not being productive, they might think it's selfish, but taking care of ourselves gives us the capacity to take care of other peoaple, and if we don't do it, we burn out. So I like to remind people all the time about how important it is.*
>
> —Diana Winston, Director, UCLA Mindfulness Education (2023) Schmidt, Brie. "TikTok's 'filler Episode' Days Are More than a Trend - They're the Reprieve You Need." *Glam,* Glam, 21 May 2023, www.glam.com/1292052/tiktok-filler-episode-days-mental-health-benefits/.

> *Your main character energy deserves a day (or more) of recovery.*

Not every single day can be a day to enact systemic change and be doing the most. You need filler episode days. Let your mind wander and allow yourself to daydream. "Mind-wandering can enable prospective cognitive operations that are likely to be useful to the individual as they navigate through their daily lives" (Baird, Smallwood, and Schooler, 2011, p. 1604).

Not every episode needs to have the excitement of a dramatic plot line. Give yourself the grace to have a day where you can unwind, refuel, and self-resource in a way that is nourishing for you after a big plot line–type of day.

Filler episodes are episodes where nothing particularly eventful happens. The storyline won't impact the overall plot and may even be a break from other intense story arcs that have been playing out in the show that is your own life. Consider taking time for integration. As you continue participating with the learnings and invitations in this text, emotions may arise for you to tend to and sit with. As you explore your role in this work and this world, your body will be in the process of integrating these personal realizations. Remember the permission slip you wrote for yourself in the beginning of the book. Consider giving yourself permission to have filler episodes where seemingly nothing exciting or momentous occurs.

Figure 12.2

Have fun.

It might be odd to be reading this line in the systemic change section and also around being autonomous. But the most important way you can radically disrupt the system is by prioritizing your joy as an individual within a system that was explicitly designed with your joy on the farthest back of the back burners. Any system robbing you of the opportunity to create, to improvise, to play, and to claim authentic joy is robbing you of the opportunity for healing. Fun is healing. Fun is pattern interrupting. Fun is revolutionary. Give yourself an opportunity to explore having fun in new ways. Giving the brain new experiences and the curiosity of newness and the unfamiliar invites us to interrupt monotony. There has to be newness and unfamiliarity to systemic change; it's all about recognizing that we are doing things *differently* than before.

13

Focusing on What You Know Is Right

One day during lunch, I was microwaving my food in the teachers' lounge and couldn't tell how many seconds were left because of the roaches crawling in front of the numbers. I realized two things at that moment. First, I probably should start packing cold lunches. (Check out the versatile lunch recipe found in Part IV.) And second, how has this become so normal that my colleagues aren't disgusted and outraged? This level of "toxic" in our work environment has become normalized. Once home, I decided to write a Facebook post about my lunch break experience, and it went viral . . . overnight.

The next morning I was called into the principal's office. "Someone has to take a hit for this, Thomas" is what my administrator told me. And it turns out that the person who was taking the hit was me. For speaking up. For using my voice. For sharing my norm with the world who helped to wake me up in the realization that this wasn't okay. My post went viral because of the shock factor of my current reality; however, the shock factor is not even necessary to spark systemic change.

But my personal shock was around my realization that *a teacher's working conditions are a student's learning conditions.* And if our students are learning in a culture based in fear, then we aren't truly serving students, are we? According to Maslow's hierarchy of needs, students who feel unsafe are not able to reach the highest levels of learning and self-actualization. And (drumroll please) the same applies to adults, too! If teachers and other adult staff members are consumed with fear and do not feel safe, we aren't able to reach those higher levels of self-actualization, either. Additionally, it may be hard to see that leadership is often trapped in the same constraints that teachers are. Many times the administration is grappling with the same issues and seemingly insurmountable roadblocks as teachers.

Often the patterns of injustices are insidious and normalized, which makes them even more subversive. Sometimes we don't even question the way things are because they're just "the way things are." But now, more than ever, we must question and rise up against the system that has been built to intentionally disempower certain genders, cultural backgrounds, and professions. The system is also built to keep fear alive and to keep us small. Focus on what you know is right, not on your fears.

The next section not only acknowledges the economic, social, and political issues that shape our working conditions (and students' learning conditions) but also provides steps and action items to disrupt unjust systems. This chapter is about following your gut instinct, your soul's purpose, and finding others who believe in the same. There is strength in numbers and power in community. One can collectively organize within a preexisting framework by leaning on the resources that already exist or even start a framework from scratch at the grassroots level.

The concept behind this section moves beyond the individual and pushes for change for *everyone* at school. Turning up the volume around working toward a collective solution creates systemic change. Instead of looking at just your own individual issues, ask yourself: How am I pushing back on overarching problems? It's not just about protecting yourself but rather focusing on collective liberation. How can you try to be useful in making your community a better place?

WORK TO CHANGE THAT WHICH HARMS STUDENTS

Why are we adopting structures and systems that are oppressive? If a structure or system makes you feel icky, know that it just shouldn't make you feel that way.
—Ashley Esposito, Baltimore City, Maryland, School Board Member

VIDEO 13.1

School Board Member and social change activist Ashley Esposito shares helpful tips and information to enact systemic change.

https://www.wiley.com/go/happyteacherrevolution

Work intentionally to change school policies and systems that hurt students. Write letters, protest, schedule meetings with policymakers, take action. And if those steps fail, act with righteous indignation even if the system tells you that you're wrong. Often the system in place exists because it hasn't been challenged and truly benefits those in power, even if its beneficiaries are not overtly obvious. An eighth-grade Social Studies Teacher in Collinsville, Illinois, shared with me, "I confide in a trusted coworker or union rep to be sure I did nothing wrong then ask for a meeting with the principal. Sometimes when feeling trapped, an email copied to those involved or a day off helps." Ashley in Baltimore makes the following suggestion: "If you are able to, contact someone anonymously if possible. If you don't feel comfortable talking to the principal, keep it confidential and share with someone who may not be in the school directly who doesn't have skin in the game." Consider the various channels to plant these seeds of disruption. Be the squeaky wheel. Form allyships with those who are also disruptors. Trust and rest in the goodness of what you are doing and acknowledge that your instincts, intuition, and gut has led you to this very moment and to the truth in your "knowing" that has led you to read this text right now.

Transforming education cannot happen without a recognition that it is a system that has taken on colonial structures that oppress Indigenous folks and does the same with urban youth. . . . We must snatch the image of

> *anti-intellectualism of youth of color . . . from the district office, the school, the classroom—even while recognizing there will be challenges and obstacles as we engage in this process. . . . One does not depart from the teacher training one received in the university or school district and not expect some resistance. However, if the goal is freedom, a departure is essential.*
>
> —Emdin (2021, p. 102)

The structures in place in traditional classrooms do not lend themselves to giving either students or teachers a voice or a space in which to be valued and respected for their experiences. The system was not designed to amplify the voices of students and teachers; even more, it is actively suppressing the voices of those in historically marginalized communities.

The method that you use doesn't have to be flashy to get it done . . . it's the idea of standing up for something that is in service of the collective.

If you experience pushback yourself, that's a sign that your work is working.

Know that if there is a pushback, it's an opportunity to embrace the shifts you are making in terms of systemic change. Resistance is a sign of the work working. The system benefits when you stay silent, continue to uphold the traditions, and do not collectively organize with fellow change makers. Acknowledge that systemic change is inconvenient, especially for those maintaining the status quo. This does not mean we assimilate; rather it means that we continue to uphold our fight for equity as we advocate for positive change. Revolutionary transformation has a collective impact, and resistance is part of the journey.

GET COMFORTABLE WITH BEING UNCOMFORTABLE

Advocating for myself has been a more recent priority for me in these most recent years. I try to avoid standing out although being six foot and one of the few male teachers in my school makes it challenging to be Waldo. It took starting the journey of personal and professional development for me to realize that it's crucial to speak up because my thinking could potentially be an asset to discovering a solution to a problem. Being overly critical of my thoughts and opinions doesn't help the situation or improve the learning environment as an educator and certainly prolongs my improvement as a person.

> *I reflect on the exercise of what is the worst that can happen when determining to act on what is the right thing to do. It's setting realistic expectations of what is the worst result when acting on something that makes me nervous. With my own experience of moving past the fear, I can proudly say that I feel better knowing that I stepped out of my comfort zone and was able to accomplish something.*
>
> —Ricardo C., ESL Teacher, Deer Park, New York

In terms of creating change, acknowledge that discomfort is part of the revolutionary act of systemic upheaval. In the research study "Motivating Personal Growth by Seeking Discomfort," Woolley and Fishbach (2022) found that "seeking discomfort is motivating because people can tell when they feel uncomfortable and this 'tangible feeling' of discomfort can lead to goal progress" (quoted in Magnus-Sharpe, 2022).Consider all of the times in your life when change felt incredibly uncomfortable and unfamiliar. Knowing that there is a level of discomfort that is to be expected—not only expected but *encouraged*—can help to reframe the situation as a personal growth opportunity. Consider the perspective of the students within your very own community and the brand-new material that you introduce as an educator. Connecting to this experience of discomfort that you've experienced in new situations and circumstances can help you to better understand your students but also better understand yourself, too.

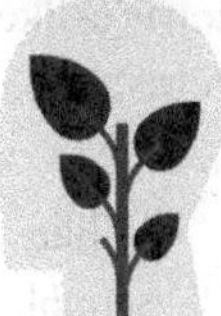

> *There's nothing more dangerous than someone who wants to make the world a better place.*
>
> —Banksy (2021)

TRY THIS: DIG FOR DATA

Data speaks volumes. Is there exit survey data in your community that identifies the perspectives of teachers who are leaving and why they left? Are there anonymous climate and culture surveys that contain data that can be extrapolated to back your point? Data doesn't lie, and it can be a source of opportunity to initiate systemic change. It also can become a reference for systemic change, taking the "personal" components out of the conversation.

MANAGE YOUR EXPECTATIONS

As a school librarian, I do believe that intellectual freedom will prevail over fascism in the end. In elementary school, we don't deal with a lot of book banning nonsense, which I'm thankful for. But, I think having an up-to-date selection policy and challenge policy that are accessible to all is important. We're very fortunate to have progressive leaders in our school system. I think overall the attacks on intellectual freedom actually shoot the perpetrators in the foot because NO ONE I know ever had any opinions on critical race theory, and now everyone is talking about it. It actually pushes progressives to double down on teaching critically and protecting our students' rights to read!

—Keeli, Librarian, Nashville, Tennessee

Pushing back on an issue at school that is not right that impacts kids negatively, whether it is a discriminating dress code policy, what's being served in the cafeteria, or curriculum that isn't developmentally appropriate, takes time and may not happen overnight. Manage your expectations around the time it takes for systemic change to occur. As the founder of a global movement to support the mental health and well-being of educators, our Revolutionaries like Keeli have encouraged fellow members to consider the potential short-term and long-term benefits of advocating for systemic change.

> While classroom teachers can certainly impact the culture of a school, there are often structural issues that cannot be resolved by one person. These problems exist because they are systemic in nature. They require the redistribution of power within the organization. Classroom educators have a responsibility to participate in this work and advocate for more inclusive and equitable learning environments; however, systemic work and shifting a community's culture takes time. (Kleinrock, 2021, p. 77)

Although leaders and policymakers may be on board with systemic change and believe they are doing meaningful work to dismantle existing unjust structures, these initiatives must be "scrutinized for surface-level performativity and for whether or not they are based on deficit ideologies" (Kleinrock, 2021, p. 76). Shiny, quick-fix, performative Band-Aid fixes to systemic change may seem to be easy wins or solutions, but true systemic change takes significant time.

Moving the needle may be a relatively slow process. Representative John Lewis devoted his life to racial justice and equality, and during a 2016 House of Representatives sit-in following the Pulse shooting in Orlando, FL, he shared, "We have been too quiet for too long. There comes a time when you have to say something. You have to make a little noise. You have to move your feet. This is the time" (quoted in Smith and Woolf, 2016).

Ask for forgiveness instead of permission.

All kinds of visible or invisible signs may say "Do not do take this path. Do not advocate for change," but consider what the actual repercussions will be. While I am not saying to risk your own safety and security, I do acknowledge that the authoritative, fear-based leadership so commonly seen in unhealthy educational environments hinges on the assumption that you will stay docile and silent. What if you choose to act from a place of empowerment toward systemic change rather than asking for permission to enact such change? What's the worst that could happen? Weigh your outcomes and consider asking for forgiveness instead of permission.

IDENTIFY THE FEAR

I've worked through the ups and downs of teaching by working through my fear. Fear can keep us safe, but it can often keep us very small.

—Nancy Y., Middle School Science Teacher, New Jersey

Identify the difference between fear for survival versus fear of taking up space and being seen. The first step in discerning the two types of fear is self-awareness. Name and identify the fear. Name what is happening in your body. Actually list the physical sensations. Does your heart race? Are your palms sweaty? Is your breathing shallow? Is your jaw tight? Next self-reflect. Consider whether this is fear for your survival or, instead, a fear around standing up for yourself or against corrupt systems.

Although research shows we have gained some important knowledge of the mechanisms of obedience, unfortunately "we are left with little understanding about the nature of disobedience to unjust authority—an act that is a precondition for social progress" (Bocchiaro, Zimbardo, and Van Lange, 2012, p. 45).

While passive bystanders often outnumber active ones, studies also show that people who take a chance and act aren't dramatically different, personality-wise, from the rest of the population (Darley and Latané, 1968). They aren't necessarily more outgoing or daring than the average personality type (Svoboda, 2019).

Acknowledge that while it may feel uncomfortable, you have the ability to be an active bystander rather than a passive bystander within your own life. Standing up for what is right may be more worthwhile and empowering than prioritizing obedience within an unjust system.

TRY THIS: CHOOSE YOUR BATTLES

Consider where the fear is coming from and prioritize your own knowing rather than the influence of others. Remember, continue to offer yourself grace, self-compassion, and permission to what you will or will not spend your energy on. Or, as we say in the Happy Teacher Revolution community, "I choose the battles worth fighting." Give yourself permission to set boundaries with parents, students, the administration, and yourself. Make the conscious choice to be an active participant in your own life and consider what it might look like to push past the discomfort of choosing your sense of justice rather than a commitment to obedience.

IDENTIFY IMPERFECTION VERSUS DYSFUNCTION

A revolution cannot occur in isolation . . . there are tons of messy imperfections in teaching. But there is a difference between imperfection and dysfunction.

—Meredith N., High School English Teacher, North Carolina

VIDEO 13.2

Meredith, who has taught in multiple states around the country, shares an authentic perspective around her journey in education

https://www.wiley.com/go/happyteacherrevolution

I CHOOSE THE
battles worth
FIGHTING
HAPPY TEACHER REVOLUTION.

Figure 13.1

While it is important that we manage our expectations around an absolutely *perfect* work environment, there is something to be said for following one's own instincts when it comes to taking action regarding a dysfunctional work environment.

Wide evidence indicates that employees have valid reasons to fear coming out to their supervisor when they cannot trust their reaction, even when working in an overall positive organizational climate (Dolan, Capell, Tzafrir, and Enosh, 2014). First, due to elements of power in the relationship, mistreatment or hostility by a supervisor takes a heavy toll on employees' well-being, especially when an employee is singled out (Huo, Lam, and Chen 2012; Langan-Fox, Cooper, and Klimoski 2007; Tepper et al., 2009).

Fear plays a huge role in one's course of action, so consider an opportunity to connect with colleagues and rally together to avoid being singled out by those in a position of authority. When it comes to a dysfunctional work environment, rely on strength in numbers when taking action.

Give yourself permission to follow what is right. Focus on soul-care, not just self-care.

Consider Meredith's advice: Be the *you* that you are without trying to force it. The *you* that you are is inspiration to your liberation. It's not about feeling trapped, it's about feeling liberated. As you continue your journey, whatever that looks like, you get to follow the wisdom of your soul rather than the system. Loving teaching begins with loving yourself, and when you do practice active self-love, your students have the opportunity to pick up on that positive soul-energy, they begin to feel safe, and they become 21st-century thinkers and problem solvers.

CREATE COMMUNITY

You have to do what's right even if you don't think there will be an audience for what is right. In order to engage teachers around mental health, we need to have conversations with practitioners, researchers, and people in the field so we can figure out what are the best ways to help support educators. And when I say that I'm not just speaking of teachers. . . . I'm speaking about principals, anyone in education, pre-K through 12, and higher education.

—Fran, former Educator and Founder of
Teacher Self-Care Conference, Atlanta, Georgia

VIDEO 13.3

Fran describes the importance and implications of engaging educators around themes of mental health and well-being as a necessary component of systemic change.

https://www.wiley.com/go/happyteacherrevolution

This is the part where I reiterate that this is *not* an us versus them scenario when it comes to teachers versus administrators. Being a disruptor is an equal opportunity that transcends the silos, boxes, and labels we are placed in within the education system. We're in this together. We have an opportunity to create a community aligned to a higher purpose around doing "education" differently, and not just keeping with the same old traditions because "that's just the way it's always been." Create a sense of community, even if it starts with just you.

Recent research suggests that for institutional change to succeed, change agents within an institution need to form and maintain communities of like-minded individuals (Pitterson, Allendoerfer, Streveler, Ortega-Alvarez, and Smith, 2020). The structures that inhibit transformational change for educators are the same structures that leaders are operating within, too. Fostering a community aligned to a higher purpose is our chance to rally individuals from different backgrounds, locations, roles, and responsibilities into a larger collective.

Keep going.

Keep going, even if others don't see the value of it. Be a forward thinker and connect with experts whose research aligns with your advocacy. It may be scary to be the first one to speak up, so consider seconding a colleague or cosigning a petition to enact change. Often the ones who are at the forefront of using their voices to enact systemic change within a community can feel isolated or alone in their endeavors, so consider backing up those who have stuck their necks out to make necessary shifts for collective transformation. Keep going.

AMPLIFY YOUR AUTHENTIC SELF

Your students are legit starting to explore their own voice in a way that either furthers survivorship or enters them into thriveship. It's integral that you are walking in your own fire, showing them leadership can look and take on varying forms.

—Taylor Gonzalez, former Second-Grade Teacher, Fort Lauderdale, Florida

Perhaps the most disruptive way of enacting systemic change is by being *yourself.* As Emdin (2016, p. 35) says:

> When I took my first job in a school with students whose faces looked much like mine, the most memorable advice I received from an older teacher was, "You look too much like them, and they won't take you seriously. Hold your ground, and don't smile till November." To be an effective black male educator for youth of color, I was being advised to erase pieces of myself and render significant pieces of who I was invisible. That's what was needed to enter into teaching, which was increasingly being presented as a war against young people.

Instead of erasing pieces of yourself, highlight, underline, bold, and italicize them!

Emdin believes that the mantra "Don't smile till November" encourages teachers to erase themselves and their emotions while working with students. It turns the collective of passionate educators into automatons with a sole focus of maintaining the school's structures and inequities. Rather than facing our fears, this mantra masks them. And because being in touch with one's emotions is the key to moving from the classroom (place) to the spaces where the students are, if we hide our emotions, our students end up being invisible to us.

The point is not to force teachers and students to be part of the dominant systemic culture but rather to move everyone to be themselves together. The current education system rewards both students and teachers who blindly assimilate; a homogenous student identity in which everyone assimilates into a set of school norms is celebrated, despite the fact that doing so requires students and teachers to repress their authentic selves (Emdin, 2016).

Personal Growth

Once we encourage populations that have been systematically marginalized to be their authentic selves, they make deep connections with their teachers, their fellow students, and the learning process (Emdin, 2016). Right now, there's a big push for bad things, whether it's bad curriculum, bad policies, or others. You may have experienced explicit indoctrination when you entered into the system, and you may have learned to follow protocols that may be harmful to the mental health and well-being of others in the interest of helping kids. Now that you know it is hurting them, you don't need to do it anymore. You may have been advised not to smile, not to differentiate the curriculum, not to incorporate your individuality into instruction; this is your opportunity to create systemic change by taking the first step of making significant parts of yourself visible in the work.

Being yourself may not sound like radical systemic change, but acknowledge it as the first step for yourself, your colleagues, and your students.

BREAK STUFF AND REBUILD IT

You can make modifications to a system but you'll only make small incremental changes. By changing one thing, you can rupture something somewhere else like a negative butterfly effect. In my community work, neighborhood associations have a scope of work to interact with the system at large, and we make them investigate why it is that way and most people do what they're told and never think about how to do it more efficiently or equitably.

—Ashley Esposito, Baltimore City, Maryland, School Board Member

Sometimes the best solution is to start from scratch. Perhaps instead of working within a crumbling system, we instead reimagine what it could like in an entirely new way. Create a brain dump of all possible outside-the-box–type approaches. Or consider investing time in following the human-centered design process, which posits that users/participants are experts in their own experiences, and then design solutions around their needs (National Institute of Standards and Technology, 2021). Human-centered design is a creative process dedicated to understanding people's needs and designing interventions that better serve those needs. Typically, the process includes the seven steps: (1) frame and plan; (2) research;

(3) synthesize; (4) ideate; (5) prototype; (6) implement; and (7) iterate. For our purpose in Happy Teacher Revolution, I've simplified the process into four steps:

1. Understand the issue.
2. Identify insights.
3. Brainstorm the positive.
4. Make it tangible.

Identify a common issue, not just a niche issue.

Ashley encourages us to consider the community as a whole rather than a singular individual. Also, take yourself out of it. Don't say things like "*my* kid or *my* neighborhood needs ___." Rather, consider making statements around the collective need. When it comes to systemic change, the impact is meant to help the collective community. Understand the culture and context of the problem by understanding the culture and context of the people involved. Talk to, observe, and learn from stakeholders to locate needs and assets to support. Consider these questions: *Who are my users/participants? Who will be in the community?*

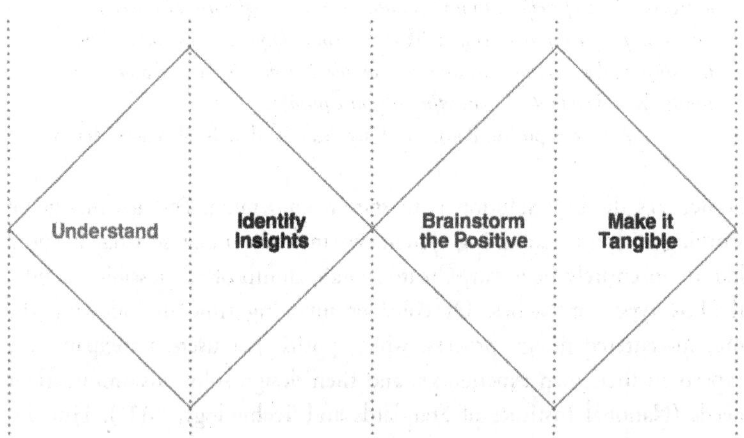

Figure 13.2 Human Centered Design Process adapted by Happy Teacher Revolution.

How can I learn about their experiences? Then, to identify insights, compile your observations and research findings and look for common themes. Find appropriate opportunities for intervention. Embrace unexpected insight, ideas, and inspiration. Ask yourself: *What are the users'/participants' needs? What patterns keep showing up? What can be intentionally designed to address this issue, even if it begins with small, incremental changes?*

Figure 13.3

14

Addressing Vicarious Trauma

Social connection builds resilience, and resilience helps create post-traumatic wisdom, and that wisdom leads to hope. Hope for you and hope for others witnessing and participating in your healing, hope for your community.

— Bruce D. Perry and Oprah Winfrey, *What Happened to You?* (2021, p. 203)

The first time I was introduced to the concept of vicarious or second-hand trauma, I was sitting in a college lecture class titled "The Arts and Medicine." The course about the interconnectedness among the brain, the arts, and healing was taught by one of the incredible educators who truly saved my life, George Sampson, at the University of Virginia. George supported me during a time of crisis by making accommodations so that I could not only make it to graduation but could continue to choose life. He is the reason I'm able to be here right now to convey that message to you, precious reader.

I remember sitting in the lecture hall in George's class and learning that mental health professionals who support individuals who have experienced trauma (whether it be surviving domestic abuse or a natural disaster, witnessing an act of violence, or any number of things) are very closely monitored themselves. Why? Because those mental health professionals can develop vicarious trauma as a result of their professional work, even though they never directly witnessed or experienced any of the traumatic incidents shared by their patients. This moment in George's course was a huge light bulb experience for me, but it made an even more visceral impact when I started my journey as an educator myself.

Thankfully, the fact that this concept was discussed in college proves that there has been a positive evolution in the education system, which has adapted to be more trauma informed (or at least trauma aware). But even though I was introduced to the concept of vicarious trauma in college, there was a surprising lack of exposure to the concept of vicarious or secondhand trauma in my graduate coursework. It wasn't until I became "Miss Thomas" that I realized how ill prepared I was for the emotional demands of the job, specifically the emotional demands unique to supporting individuals who have experienced trauma firsthand. And what's unique about this population is that they are children.

We've already covered what it looks like to support our students or other individuals who have experienced trauma, but I believe an important and often unnamed component is supporting the caregivers. This is the key to systemic change and the system overhaul that is absolutely necessary to be more trauma informed and thus more effective holistically.

Before I go any further, you are never *ever* required to reimagine or alchemize a traumatic experience as an opportunity. Rather, I invite you to design your own roadmap for your own unique personal journey that highlights your agency and power when dealing with systemic change and supporting caregivers experiencing secondhand trauma.

Tune In to the Wisdom of Your System

When we are disconnected from our bodies, we are also disconnected from the ability to tune in to the important information being sent from the body to the brain through the vagal pathway. . . . [T]he ability to flexibly move between states is a sign of well-being and resilience. It is when we are

> *caught in dysregulation, unable to find our way back to regulation, that we feel distress.*
>
> —Deb Dana, LCSW, *Anchored: How to Befriend Your Nervous System Using Polyvagal Theory* (Sounds True, 2021, p. 30)

The "vagal" in polyvagal theory refers to the vagus nerve,

> which in fact is not a single nerve but rather a bundle of nerves that begin in the brainstem and travel through the body, affecting many different organs along the way. *Vagus* means "wanderer" in Latin, and because of the length of this nerve (the vagus is the longest cranial nerve) and the ways it connects in so many places along its route, it seems it is appropriately named. (Dana, 2021, p. 28)

I love the connection of this etyomology to this book's title and invite you to give yourself permission to be a wanderer on the path to well-being. Consider the neurobiological vagal pathway as the literal route to claiming and sustaining well-being.

I learned about polyvagal theory while experiencing what a regulated nervous system is firsthand. At the same time, I realized that the goal of having a regulated nervous system is not the unrealistic expectation that I'm at a level of perfect Zen peacefulness all the time . . . but rather it is the space where we can hold the uncomfortable moments WITH joy instead of without it altogether. Self-compassion is essential in moments that are challenging, especially when we acknowledge those uncomfortable feelings.

Instead of ignoring them and pretending that stressful moments don't exist, or getting angry and rageful at situations outside of our control, make the deliberate decision to reclaim the power of listening to your body and learning to tune in to the wisdom of the nervous system.

Consider glimmers versus triggers.

Deb Dana, licensed clinical social worker and author who specializes in complex trauma, uses the term "glimmers" in her work with polyvagal theory (2021, p. 115). Glimmers can help to spark joy and restore inner calm. Embracing glimmers can be a transformative way to see the world surrounding us. In these micro-moments where we feel a spark of ventral energy and are anchored in safety,

HAPPY TEACHER REVOLUTION

GUIDE TO GLIMMERS

ADAPTED FROM DEB DANA, LCSW, "ANCHORED: HOW TO BEFRIEND YOUR NERVOUS SYSTEM USING POLYVAGAL THEORY" (SOUNDS TRUE, 2021). PRINTED WITH PERMISSION.

- Glimmers are the opposite of triggers.
- They are micro-moments that shape our nervous system.
- They cue our nervous system to feel safe or calm.
- Glimmers help our biology be in a place of connection or regulation
- They are bite-size but contribute to our well-being in a big way.
- They have a positive effect on mental health.

Happy Teacher Revolution:
The Educator's Roadmap to Claiming & Sustaining Joy

Figure 14.1 The Happy Teacher Revolution guide to glimmers. Adapted from Deb Dana, LCSW, *Anchored: How to Befriend Your Nervous System Using Polyvagal Theory* (Sounds True, 2021). Printed with permission.

we are better able to connect with others and with ourselves. It's easy to miss glimmers if we aren't looking, especially because of humans' built-in negative biases. In order to survive, we are wired to respond more intensely to negative experiences. Thus, we must be intentional to actively look for and keep track of these tiny glimmers that foster safety and connection. Also, finding glimmers doesn't negate the experiences of intensity or stress. Rather, we can be in the messy middle, holding both uncertainty and safety alongside the bright spots.

CHECK IN WITH YOURSELF AND KNOW YOU AREN'T ALONE

> *Be confident enough to know that you are not the only one who has gone through this and that should almost feel like a sigh of relief knowing that there are people who have also gone through similar situations that you might have gone through. . . . Keep the lens of the learner. Keep the mindset of I'm just starting off and learning something new and that's okay. I'm supposed to be exploring and curious.*
>
> —Ricardo, ESL Teacher, Deer Park, NY

VIDEO 14.1

Ricardo describes the importance of being present and checking in with yourself as a reflective practice that support our individual well-being.

https://www.wiley.com/go/happyteacherrevolution

Acting autonomously doesn't equate to being abandoned or isolated. In fact, it's just the opposite. When you take a stand for yourself and for systemic change and refuse to abandon yourself and your values, you aren't left out in the cold. Rather, it shows you with whom you are clearly aligned and who supports your sense of sovereignty.

Reimagine resilience.

Psychologists have coined the term "hedonistic treadmill" to describe a never-ending chase toward the next best thing to achieve joy and reach pure unadulterated happiness. The perpetual rat race only exhausts us on the chase toward something that is impossible. I argue that we should invest in the present moment, tend to our nervous systems, and cultivate awareness around the full spectrum of the human experience, not just the shiny, polished, filtered feelings. In fact, there's recently been a development in the understanding of our sixth sense called interoception, which is the deep interconnection between the brain and body (Price and Hooven, 2018). Since the nervous system is always recording what is going on in the body, fostering support around interoception helps us cultivate awareness of ourselves.

The practice of resilience is coming back to the practice.

—Maya B., former Dance Educator and Embodiment Facilitator, Baltimore, MD

What if resilience is rest? What if resilience is grieving? What if resilience is being allowed to be human? In cultivating a more resilient version of yourself, consider that the secret ingredient to resilience is doing *less*. Hustle culture and the toxic narrative glorifying the grind is not accidental; it is born from a place of viewing human beings as human *doings*. Rather than operating as if you are a robot or Energizer bunny, consider cyclical or seasonal living. Consider this an invitation to listen to your body as you move through the world and notice seasons where you crave rest, spaciousness, and time for integration. The practice itself is continuing to repeatedly engage in these moments of embodied somatic experiences. Nothing in nature is ever constantly blooming.

Align your work, your life, your way to design this life on a rhythm and cycle that's also aligned for you. For me, this means knowing/helping to predict days I may be a little more introverted and days when I want to connect and be more outward facing. Being present in your own body is systemic change in action, as we often don't pay attention to or tend to our bodies with a sense of our own well-being in mind.

What You Witness, You Need to Bear Witness To

Compassion allows us to bear witness to suffering, whether it is in ourselves or others, without fear; it allows us to name injustice without hesitation, to act strongly, with all the skill at our disposal.

—Sharon Salzberg, *Lovingkindness: The Revolutionary Art of Happiness* (2004, p. 88)

VIDEO 14.2

Trauma specialist Becky Haas describes the importance of taking time to recharge as a trauma-informed practice.

https://www.wiley.com/go/happyteacherrevolution

Earlier in the book I mentioned the importance of bearing witness to the experiences of others by being an appreciative listener. Consider bearing witness to your own internal landscape just as intently, as this is an important component in enacting change at the systemic level. When we are in the position of bearing witness to individuals who have experienced trauma, we are invited to also bear witness to our own selves as a starting point to true systemic change. Instead of ignoring or pretending your own needs and experiences don't exist, choose to acknowledge and be a witness to the valid grief, anger, rage, sadness, or disappointment that may be present. Bear witness to the suffering you may have experienced, if even for a brief moment.

Consider your well-being like a bank account and the moments of spending time investing in yourself as deposits into your well-being account. When you make deposits, you accrue interest, however small an amount, by normalizing this level of baseline in your personal well-being. When you are constantly showing up for others in a caregiver role, and especially when individuals you are supporting have experienced trauma themselves, it's important to remember that you are susceptible to having your account overdrawn.

In our evolution as we shed the next layer, acknowledge the tenderness underneath.

As we begin to sit with and embody the full spectrum of emotions and also acknowledge backlogged feelings, we are in a tender moment of our evolution. In that moment, there is a tenderness regarding what is newly formed and underneath what has shed. Offer yourself grace, rest, reflection, and integration in your current season of evolution. As a butterfly metamorphosizes, its wings are powerful and also delicate. You can't spell "revolution" without "evolution." In that transformation, acknowledge the power in the softness.

Plug into your charging station.

When individuals are at risk of experiencing vicarious trauma, they are also more likely to risk burnout and being overwhelmed. When we plug into our charging station, we are practicing the intentional act of unlearning what has been modeled to us. I would also extend Becky's metaphor from the video by emphasizing taking time to integrate and find spaciousness after charging. I learned recently that it's unhealthy to leave your electronics plugged in all the time; they need a break to just "be." This same metaphor applies to us in creating containers to do "nothing" and integrate both self-care and experiences of "doing" for others. We must bear witness to what shows up between the moments of charging and depletion simply to exist as ourselves.

For generations leading up to this moment, the term "burnout" has been worn as a badge of honor. Reconsidering what a "good" teacher does in practice and making this visible not only to those in our lives but as an example for our own brains to take note of is an instance of what systemic change looks like in action. Thus, we are able to course-correct the tumultuous path that the education system has led us down. We are able to redefine what it means to be a "good" teacher and to celebrate folks who prioritize their well-being rather than those who sacrifice their wholeness for the sake of the profession.

ADVOCATING FOR YOURSELF IS ADVOCATING FOR OTHERS

The more stressed and anxious we are, the less access we have to our creativity, our resilience, our stop and think practice to take a breath before iterating with a kid or colleague. It's a reminder to each other what we need to know how to do.

—Chris Moore, Ed.S. Director of Mental Health & Social-Emotional Learning and School Psychologist, Salem-Keizer Public Schools, Salem, Oregon

At the time of writing, teachers are preparing their wills prior to going back to school post-COVID 19. Being a martyr does not help anyone in the long term. Putting your own needs last hurts your students when you can't give them all that they need. Ignoring your needs until you ultimately decide to leave the classroom hurts the profession as a whole. Every time we lose someone in the field, we lose the money the school has invested and the relationships built with stakeholders. We also add stress on other folks in the building, add stress for kids in losing a caregiver within the community, and add stress on leadership to constantly search for replacements as the number of teacher vacancies skyrockets.

Research by the Energy Project indicates that if you do not put your needs first, ultimately you will not be able to perform well and show up for others consistently and happily. The project recently found that workers who didn't practice good self-care often had trouble focusing on one thing and were easily distracted (Firestone, 2017). Taking care of ourselves not only makes our personal lives better; it also makes us better able to focus on the subtleties and nuances of our students' mental, emotional, and physical needs.

The martyrdom complex is a danger in caregiving professions. It leads people to believe that, to prove their worth and to offer support, they must sacrifice their own needs for the sake of others. In fact, the opposite is true: Those of us in caregiving professions need to care for ourselves to be able to care for others. We must *be well* in order to support the well-being of others.

Reframe your thought pattern around self-care and meeting your basic needs.

15

Engaging in Self-Care with Students 3

Cultivate Emotional Wellness

Emotional wellness is the solution to the social justice issues that have plagued humans for a very long time. It is a level of intelligence that is as important as other levels of intelligence if not more so important because it directly connects to how we live in the outcome of our human future.

—Ashley Williams, former Baltimore City Public Schools Educator and Founder of Clymb

There are some systems that we need to sunset. We need to stop building upon broken systems. People over products. Relationships over everything. High tide raises all boats and when we help those who are struggling, we help everyone. Recognize and celebrate the improvement, especially post pandemic. Let's not take the joy out of teaching and learning. Don't be paralyzed by perfection. Don't let the perfect picture get in the way, disrupt the status quo.

—Superintendent, Virginia

VIDEO 15.1

Ashley shares her inspiration behind cultivating emotional wellness in order to enact greater systemic change for all of humanity.

https://www.wiley.com/go/happyteacherrevolution

Centering our collective humanity in the classroom is a way to consider the day-to-day reimagining of systemic change within the education system. You can't be trauma informed if you don't talk about the structures in place that have been perpetuating injustice and inequities. Interrogate those structures. Because we aren't conforming to the way of being or assimilating, we can model to our students what disrupting the system looks like in action. In our conversations, day-to-day interactions, and observations within the systems we operate in, consider centering humanity first and foremost. Consider your own humanness as the ultimate center.

adrienne marie brown encourages us to create a culture of celebration: "It seems simple but people stay more engaged in a space where they are enjoying each other, and feel celebrated and appreciated. Small, personal celebrations help fuel groups through the hard work, reminding them that they are humans together, regardless of the external pressures they face" (2021, p. 21). Cultivate emotional wellness by centering your humanness and engaging with the practice of acknowledging one another as human beings rather than human do-ings.

BE A LIFELONG LEARNER

Consider disassociating or reprogramming the tool/act from what it was like learning how to do the tool/act or using the tool/act. One example for me personally in my own lifelong learning has been writing. Learning how to write and communicate my thoughts was stressful when I was a student in grade school, especially because I needed remediation for my handwriting. Writing felt like it was something I was bad at because of what it looked like, not necessarily because of the content. I realized this was an invitation for me to practice the presentness of self-compassion while writing. It was a reminder that when we are beginners, whether we are learning a new skill or a new mindset/approach, it may not feel comfortable from the very beginning. Rather, just like our students learning new skills, we have the opportunity to cultivate a new way of doing and being an educator, a leader, a creator, a social innovator, and a changemaker.

Recognize that the journey to claiming and sustaining joy looks different for everyone and that we are all learning. Honor the process for how we arrive there. There may be backlogged trauma that's being processed and witnessed for the first time. Know that you are not alone and that the body may feel safe for the very first time even to experience these uploads/downloads. Continue maintaining your supports, prioritize well-being practices that support your regulated nervous system, and offer yourself grace each step of the way.

Model to your students and share transparency about your experiences as a learner. Being able to connect with your students from this perspective can help you find common ground and be a means of cultivating a big-picture point of view.

TRUST IN YOUR OWN TIMING

Consider your own lifetime and everything that has led up to this very moment right now. I am getting full-body goose bumps and chills down my back as I write because I'm feeling it for myself. There has been a chain of events that has occurred, and this message right now is a reminder of the brilliance and magnificence of you existing in this very moment. I am honored for you to consider showing up for yourself in a radical way and for the messages embedded within this resource to have been just one small reminder of your infinite light.

Part of systemic change is realizing that *you are the pattern interrupter.* You may get opportunities for certain realizations to arrive to inspire you along your journey. These may show up as symbols, repeated images or numbers, or serendipitously timed events that trigger a chain of thinking that helps you arrive at a new way of considering a solution or another approach to the larger vision or way of doing things.

Be open to observations of affirmation of your autonomy, your journey, and your individual sovereignty that are available to you as you continue one day at a time on the unique path you are on. Your timing is exactly spot on, and I invite you to notice symbols, signs, gestures, or signals that remind you of this message in your daily life. For me this may be in a saying

I hear echoed by a stranger that my grandmother used to share, the scent of lavender that reminds me of my mom, the numbers 11:11 I see on clocks or license plates, or even a song on the radio that reminds me of a person, time, or place that left a profound impact. You have the autonomy to choose your own adventure. As you forge your journey, stay mindful of the foundation of your ancestors and those who have shaped the path you get to continue on. Be open to the sense of humor of the world in which we live and those who connect with us in ways we may not anticipate. This expansive way of thinking opens us up to a multitude of opportunities and broad possibilities that we may not be aware of at this moment in time.

Autonomy

16

Establishing Boundaries 3

Prioritize Your Well-Being

Personal well-being is the radical act that supports systemic change. The most powerful way to move systemic change forward is to make sure you aren't burning yourself out in the process.

> Instead of figuring out ways to take care of ourselves and each other, social justice groups lose brilliant and committed activists to burn-out, disillusionment and poor health. As a result, movements are plagued by fragmentation, lack of reflection and discussion, and "wheel reinventing" that keeps them from moving their agendas forward. (Plyler, 2009, p. 123)

In order to enact systemic change over the long term, we (the collective) need you to show up for yourself. We need to trust that you will take the time that you need for yourself, rest, and protect the boundaries around your own well-being.

> People who consistently overextend themselves tend to oscillate between feeling resentful for saying yes and feeling guilty for saying no. As you keep saying yes, resentment keeps building. The more you say no, on the other hand, the more comfortable you get with it, and the guilt that once drove all your yeses starts to gradually subside. This is partly because of how misguided guilt so often is in the first place; it tends to be rooted in conditioning that you're responsible for other people's feelings, which you aren't. This is a charm for anyone on the path toward self-discovery. So if you find yourself standing at the crossroads of guilt and resentment, remember this and see if it aids you. (Dore, 2021, p. 163).

Prioritizing boundaries around your well-being is essential to systemic change.

Front-Load Self-Care for Activism

> *Activists also have other unique characteristics that can make them vulnerable to burnout. The very nature of activist work involves cultivating and maintaining awareness of large and overwhelming social problems, often carrying a burden of knowledge that society as a whole is unable or unwilling to face. This can lead to feelings of pressure and isolation that easily feed into burnout.*
>
> —Maslach and Gomes (2006, p. 43)

When I began the very first Happy Teacher Revolution meeting in Baltimore, I had no idea that the burnout educators were facing was only the tip of the proverbial iceberg. I also didn't realize that the risk of burnout was even higher for those actively engaged in disrupting the system. Those of us who are not only working within the education system but actively participating in advocating for systemic change experience a double whammy of potential burnout.

When I joined the Johns Hopkins University Social Innovation Lab in the fall of 2018 to compete to receive funding in the spring of 2019, I had no idea that I would bear witness to burnout in each of the social innovators I spent the year surrounded by. Whether they were supporting new moms, fellow medical professionals, the environment, or housing insecurity . . . all of these incredible leaders were grappling with their own sense of well-being and sustainability in their individual endeavors within the collective of activists. Consider your commitment to well-being necessary for systemic change to occur, and protect your boundaries around well-being relentlessly.

EXPRESS EMOTIONS CONSTRUCTIVELY

Find constructive ways to express emotions driving the movement of systemic change.

> Outrage at the profound injustices created by existing conditions has to be a wellspring of social change movements. The key question is not whether rage will continue to play a pivotal role . . . but whether and how we can consciously shape our expression of rage to serve social change. I have argued that rage is a natural and inevitable response to the trauma of powerlessness—but that in its raw and often unconscious form, powerless rage defeats effective movement building and can lead to destructive behavior. (Wineman 2003, p. 205)

The goal here isn't to eliminate rage, anger, and frustration. The goal isn't even to immediately alchemize these heavy emotions. Rather, the goal is to be able to maintain awareness of and be awake to the full spectrum of human emotions. We can express and organize feelings of anger, rage, and frustration by affirming that outrage is valid. We also get the opportunity to create action for desirable outcomes through a means that is consistent with our ends. We cannot advocate for wellness and sustainability if we do not operate from a place of wellness and sustainability ourselves.

PART VI

Reflecting/ Integrating 3

In the final stages of writing this book, I received a letter from a student out of the blue that I found to be incredibly compelling. This child took time out of their day to write a letter advocating for systemic change in support of the mental health and well-being of educators. Our students support your journey in claiming and sustaining joy.

> Dear Mrs. Danna:
>
> I am writing to you because in my time in middle and high school I have come across the same problem in most of my classes, unenthusiastic teachers. I'm not saying every single teacher is like this but there are a lot of them like this. The reason I think this topic deserves awareness is because I believe that unenthusiastic teachers are the reason that so many students are struggling and not caring in school. Also, teachers that are unenthusiastic only make the problem of students not caring about school worse. I say this because I have heard many students complain about how much they dislike their teachers and that it makes them not even want to do the work in

that teacher's class. In my opinion, this problem can be solved relatively quickly by advocating for teachers' pay, lessening the workload for teachers, and lastly that you can help teachers understand how to create balance in their lives so that they enjoy teaching.

The way I think that the first solution should be taken into action by advocating raising teachers' salaries so that teachers' salaries can match the good work that they do. The way schools can get the extra money to fund the teachers correctly for their jobs well done is by having fundraisers throughout the year so they can achieve the extra money. The next solution would be lessening the workload of teachers. The way that can be achieved is by getting rid of extra duties. Lastly, the last way that teachers can be more efficient and enthusiastic about their jobs is by giving them the tools they need to balance the workload and down time. Thank you for your time and I look forward to hearing from you soon.

Sincerely,
Anonymous High School Student, Virginia

Guided Meditation: Cultivating Joy and Collective Change

By Elayne Mendoza

Video P6.1

In the video, Elayne Mendoza offers a guided meditation to cultivate joy with the intention of inspiring collective change.

https://www.wiley.com/go/happyteacherrevolution

Take this opportunity to pause and enter the present moment wherever you are right now.

Whether that is at your desk inside of your car, or in the comfort of your home, start to feel the surface beneath you, lengthen your spine and relax your shoulders.

Start by gently closing your eyes, sensing the body, and observing how you are feeling right now.

And now focus on your breathing and begin by slowly inhaling through your nose and exhaling through your nose.

Inhale.

Exhale.

Inhale.

Exhale.

Deep breath in,

And deep breath out.

And as you continue to feel, move your awareness to your body, and soften a little bit more making room within your body to allow any heavy sensations to pass through.

Take this moment to pause and to create an opening inside of your mind for exploration.

Imagine yourself leading systemic change around the world.

What steps would you take if you were the leader of creating opportunities and transformation?

Who do you have to become for these transformations to take place?

And in order to make progress? Who do you need to communicate with?

Pause and witness what is coming up for you.

Releasing any stories, any limited beliefs. Allow your mind to really explore what is available for you.

Now I'm asking you to have faith that what has come up is speaking to you for a reason and that you are receiving this information in order to inspire the change that the world desires.

You possess the courage and devotion required to serve as an advocate for systemic change.

You have the discipline to carry out one aligned action after the other.

Breathe in.

Breathe out.

Breathe in.

Breathe out.

Last one deep breath in,

And deep breath out.

Now pause. open your eyes slowly and softly, move your toes and fingers.

Return back to reality and lead with love.

SOMATIC EMBODIMENT EXPERIENCE

VIDEO P6.2

Maya Basik, Dance Educator and Embodiment Teacher, guides us through an opportunity to be present in the physical body. This embodiment practice supports you in cultivating joy through enacting systemic change and allowing your body to feel the impact of your advocacy and action, as it ripples and permeates outward into the collective and through the systems in which we operate.

https://www.wiley.com/go/happyteacherrevolution

BREATHING EXPERIENCE

VIDEO P6.3

Keith Golden, Musician and Movement Teacher, guides us through an energizing breathing experience. This is a suggested breathing exercise to start your day, prep for a meeting, or perhaps use before a challenging part of your day.

https://www.wiley.com/go/happyteacherrevolution

SCENT EXPERIENCE

Safety note: Many essential oils are toxic to pets, and please do not ingest any essential oils.

Suggested scent example for systemic change: *Clary sage (Salvia sclarea)*

SOUNDTRACK EXPERIENCE

Additional music suggestions are available for your listening enjoyment on the official Happy Teacher Revolution Playlist on Spotify.
"Carry On" by GRiZ
"SUPERBLOOM" by MisterWives
"Resilient" by Rising Appalachia

TASTE EXPERIENCE

Self-care for me involves dessert. There. I said it. Part of what well-being looks like is savoring the true joy that life has to offer, and for me that's ice cream. One of the first jobs I ever had was scooping ice cream during the summer, and it brought me so much joy to see people enjoying themselves at The Split Banana in Staunton, VA. It's really hard to be unhappy about ice cream . . . so I want to leave you with one of my favorite dessert recipes to round out the integration experience of embodying joy on your personal journey to claiming happiness as your own.

DANNA BANANA DESSERT SURPRISE

Coconut oil
1 ripe banana sliced lengthwise
Cinnamon
Caramel sauce
Your favorite vanilla ice cream (coconut sorbet works too!)
Crushed cinnamon cookies, graham cracker, cinnamon cereal, or churros

Heat a few tablespoons of coconut oil over medium heat. Add the sliced banana to the pan and sprinkle with cinnamon. Leave it undisturbed for a bit so it can caramelize. It'll start to smell fragrant and amazing, flip over after it's caramelized and golden brown (about 2 minutes per side).

While the banana is sautéing, warm up your caramel sauce. Your caramel sauce can be either store-bought or homemade (I'm lazy and buy it premade but you can make homemade vegan caramel sauce, which includes coconut milk, coconut sugar, vanilla, and salt).

Scoop your favorite vanilla ice cream, top with caramel sauce, then the sauteed bananas, and finally sprinkle some crunchy cinnamon goodness (graham crackers, cookies, churros, etc.) on top.

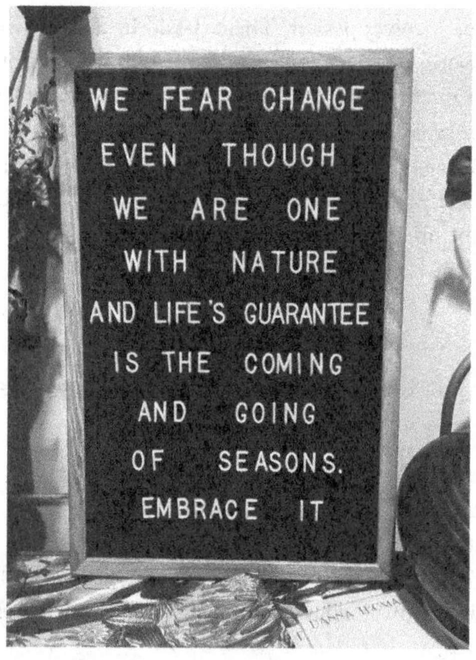

Figure P6.1 "We Fear Change."
(Lyn Patterson)

POETRY EXPERIENCE

Teaching Mental Health

I prioritize my students'
mental health
Just like they have sick days
when they have the flu,
they have mental health days
to take care of their beautiful brains
I've learned that
I set the example
for what that means
Saying "mental health"
isn't enough
I need to role model
my own mental health
and show them
what it means
to thrive in a world
that prioritizes productivity
and ableism
I hope to teach them
about their brains
but also, how to take
care of themselves
We do it together
as a community
and as a classroom

—Christina Costa, from *Kiss Your Brain: Diagnosis Diaries* (2021, pp. 42–43). Printed with permission.

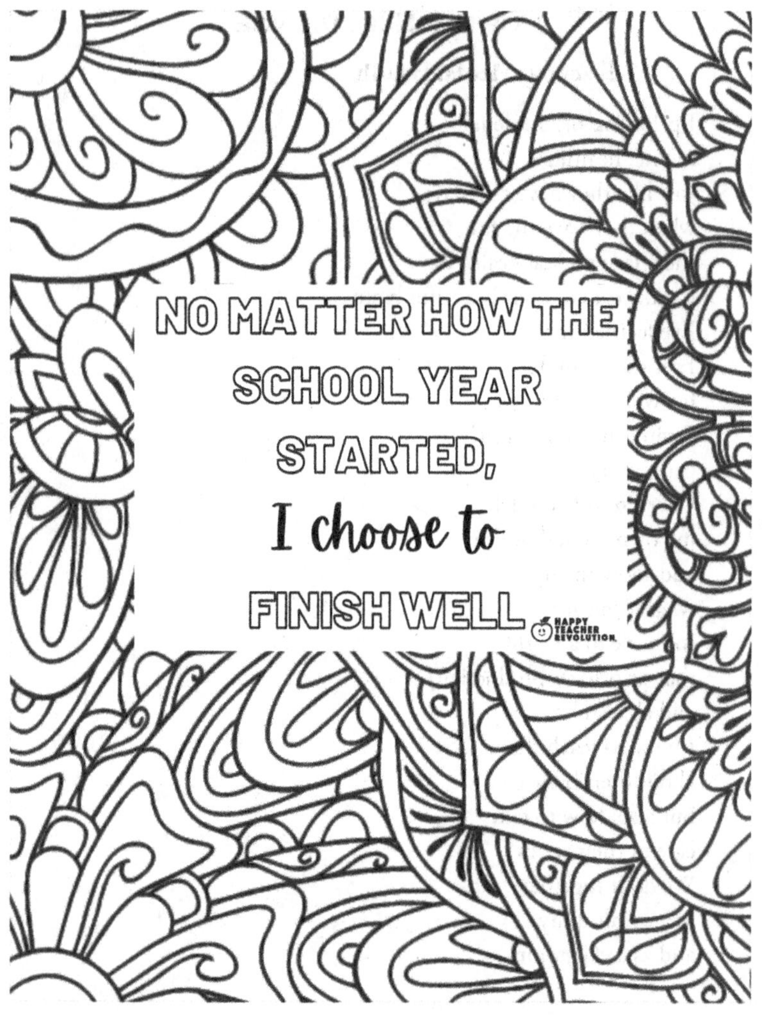
NO MATTER HOW THE
SCHOOL YEAR
STARTED,
I choose to
FINISH WELL
HAPPY TEACHER REVOLUTION

Figure P6.2

PART VII

FINALE

If you want to go east, don't go west.

—Ramakrishna

I didn't want to name this section "conclusion" or anything that had any semblance to an ending . . . because really this journey of embodying true well-being is never-ending. Just like that super-annoying song from grade school about the song that never ends, the journey of claiming joy as your own goes on and on, my friend. As a musician, the term "finale" seemed more fitting as the trumpets blared and percussion rang out in celebration of the deliberate investment you've made to show up for yourself in considering your health and happiness as absolutely essential in the work you do to serve and support others.

This meaningful role as educators and leaders is a heavy one, and also something that is equally spectacularly filled with light. I recently was describing a turning point moment to my mentor and the words "brutal" and "beautiful" came out at the same time to make "BRUTAFUL." I mean, *hello*. Isn't that exactly what life is all about combined into one word: brutaful—the gut-wrenching and breathtaking moments that are core to our being, ones that help shape the tapestry of this spectacularly colored life we get to inhabit within these magnificent bodies.

The journey of well-being, building relationships, and enacting systemic change is ongoing. As my therapist recently said, "Danna, it isn't healed or not healed. It's heal*ing*." This is an active, ongoing, practice.

The radical aspect of resilience, joy, and bliss is one that I had to reconcile within myself. Developing the skill set and adding to my tool kit of resources to tend to my well-being has not made me immune to experiencing any uncomfortable feelings. For example, when I decided to remove alcohol from my life, I thought that I would never have a brain fog moment ever again or misspeak from a place of nervous system dysregulation. Wrong. Turns out, not drinking and not participating in behavior patterns that previously numbed me have led to me being much more awake to situations. The rawness of life feels so much more visceral, and I also know with absolute confidence that I can weather this storm. I am the sky. The rest is simply the changes and evolutions in cloud formations, barometric pressure, and a natural occurring ebb and flow of the highs with the lows. Such is Mother Nature: messy, chaotic, and sometimes unexpected.

One of the realizations I've had in weaving together the colorful fabric of learnings, voicings, and experiences of the individuals throughout this book has been to reconsider moments of rejection as redirection. The number of redirections during the life span of this project has been astounding, for me both personally as an educator and as a leader in the teacher mental health space.

I started this book when I was still in the classroom. I kept writing even when I left the classroom as I became yet another statistic I was reading and researching about, particularly the pandemic of teacher burnout that existed long before the pandemic of COVID-19. Despite the almost decade of teaching under my belt and the attractive benefits of being an educator and being compensated well on the Model Teacher Pathway for Baltimore City Public Schools, I still felt a lack of support for the social-emotional demands of the job.

I drafted and redrafted the table of contents throughout each evolution of the book as I witnessed the demands placed on educators over the last six years. The glaringly obvious needs of our teachers who were so desperately crying out for support seemed clear, and yet many in positions of power continued to ignore the violence, trauma, and systemic injustices being perpetuated through a structure claiming to want "what's best for kids."

This book evolved even further when the first publishing company I was working with did not align with my values and personal principles of who I am and what this manuscript aimed to represent: diversity, inclusion, antiracism and pro equality. I refused to censor myself and even more so felt called to name the importance of supporting the well-being of LGBTQ+ educators, BIPOC educators, and any educator who has been marginalized for any reason. When we are able to stand firm in our truth and our beliefs around social justice and equality, we can pattern-interrupt systems of oppression and be a positive force in the world.

This text contains multitudes. There are only so many messages I can convey within its depths. I hope this book points you into 1 million more directions to explore and define your own understanding and sense of self. In crafting this book over the course of six years, I devoted an entire wall in my home to collecting data, quotes, soundbites, and nuggets of wisdom. It honestly looks like I was trying to track down a serial killer. And I kind of was. The serial killer was burnout, and what was being killed was our collective joy. And I was trying to get to the bottom of it.

The roadmap to your own well-being is one that is unique to you. Your detours are actually part of the trip. When the GPS tells you "recalculating," you know that this is the synchronicity of showing you toward the next path. Sometimes you may almost run out of gas, but simultaneously in these moments of crisis, there are examples of the best of humanity.

Waking up to well-being can feel more confusing and scary before it feels empowering and peaceful. Throughout the journey of this book, I've been waking up to a sense of clarity about myself and my needs within an overarching system that I hadn't felt empowered operating within. The more I invested in my well-being, the more I noticed a sense of hypervigilance within myself because my newfound sense of ease and calmness felt so unfamiliar. I realized chaos, stress, and cortisol were my comfort zones, and the grounding in the trust of my own body was what wasn't familiar. When I realized life didn't need to be spent in survival mode, I learned that my own body system is still on the journey of feeling safety in the goodness and joy of the here and now.

In writing the book on claiming your joy as a fellow educator, I have to confess that the book subtitle, *The Educator's Roadmap to Claiming & Sustaining Joy*, is a bit misleading. *You* are the one who is mapping out and journeying on the adventure toward the unknown road to claiming your own well-being. And, in doing so, the joy you experience is the joy of the full spectrum of human emotions. Joy in the shadows. Joy in the discovery. Joy in the expansion. Joy in waking up. The path to claiming (and continual intentional reclaiming) of joy is not linear. It's swirling, spiraling, and multifaceted. Consider the reclamation of joy as the reclamation of each and every shade, hue, and flavor of the human experience, similar to the swirling rainbow dots on the cover of this book. This is only the beginning.

Let's continue to show up for ourselves and each other by continuing on the journey of well-being. Consider me your copilot rooting for you every step of the way. You are seen. You are held. You are known. Thank you for showing up for yourself and opening to the wisdom of this radical, revolutionary community. We accept you and value your expertise in your own experience exactly as you are. Let the love, peace, and joy of the Happy Teacher Revolution movement help you continue your path that is so uniquely *you.*

And so I would like to end with one final message that's a call and response we say together to close every Happy Teacher Revolution gathering: *You can't pour from an empty bowl . . . you can't teach from an empty soul.*

Figure P7.1

Figure P7.2

Figure P7.3

ABOUT THE AUTHOR

Danna Thomas is a former Baltimore City Public School teacher and current founder of Happy Teacher Revolution, a global movement to support the mental health and well-being of educators. After experiencing severe depression, anxiety, and panic attacks as a student, Danna credits her own teachers as her "emotional first responders" who encouraged her to seek treatment and choose life. Her organization, Happy Teacher Revolution, is on a mission to provide the time and space for educators to feel, deal, and be real about the social-emotional demands they face on the job. Danna served as the national spokeswoman for the Music for Mental Health campaign and the National Alliance of Mental Illness (NAMI) Maryland. She is the recipient of the Johns Hopkins Community Hero Award and the 2019 Winner of the Johns Hopkins Social Innovation Lab. Danna enjoys playing the saxophone and living on her converted school bus, "Begonia," as she continues her own journey to claiming and sustaining joy.

Visit https://www.happyteacherrevolution.com to learn more about Danna and her work.

Follow her on Instagram @HappyTeacherRevolution.

ACKNOWLEDGMENTS

I first would like to thank my students. Thank you for the utmost privilege of being able to be your teacher during our time together and for the immense amount of learning that I had from being able to spend time with you and your families. I would also like to thank Tobey Antao, you were the first person to ever believe in me as an author and believed in this book before I ever believed in it myself. To the teachers who were my emotional first-responders when I was a student: Sandra Balderson, Barbara Gorrow, Matt Heist, Gregory Orr, George Sampson, Jeff Antoniuk, John D'earth, Jeff Decker, and Pete Spaar. Thank you for saving my life.

To my colleagues and changemakers mentioned throughout this text, thank you for teaching me alongside the other students that you teach in your life. I wouldn't have been able to share the messages of so many voices if you weren't so vulnerable and open in sharing your authentic truth with me and I feel so privileged to be able to amplify your stories.

To Mom and Pop, you were my very first and original teachers. Thank you for supporting me through each evolution and season, I am so grateful I get to be your daughter. To my brother, Eric, thank you for showing me what it looks like in action to absolutely love your job and the importance of bringing joy to the work that you do. To Megan, thank you for being my biggest cheerleader throughout this process and for being such a meaningful part of this collective movement. To my entire family, thank you for being an anchoring presence for me during the stormy seas and during the smooth sailing, too.

To my friends and my support network of well-being providers, thank you for helping to take care of a caregiver. I have never felt more authentically myself than I do writing this right now, and I am so proud that I got to create this resource about well-being from a resourced place of well-being. Thank you for reminding me of my light during the times when I didn't see it myself.

To Jim Hamilton and the Church on the Square community, thank you for welcoming me personally with open arms, embracing this radical concept to start a support group for teachers, and for being the very first Happy Teacher Revolution meeting site in the history of our existence. Thank you to the University of Virginia and the Jefferson Scholarship Foundation, the Johns Hopkins School of Education, the Johns Hopkins Social Innovation Lab, Teach For America, and Towson University for preparing me to launch and lead a global movement.

To our first large-scale Happy Teacher Revolution pilot sites in Colorado, Oregon, Pennsylvania, Texas, New York, and Maryland who so courageously invested in their community's well-being and systemic change while also collecting data to demonstrate impact: thank you for disrupting systems of injustice and modeling to other districts what real systemic change looks like in action.

To Ashante, my team at Jossey-Bass, the reviewers who helped shape this work into what it is today, and especially KJN: thank you all for being the reason this dream has become a reality. Your belief in me and your expertise has helped make realize a piece of art that I'm so proud to have birthed into the world to help support fellow educators. Thank you for making me feel so held, supported, and tended to as I shared my message and creative vision.

And finally, I would like to acknowledge the spirit of this very book. The process of creating this has been a coming home to myself, a deep connection with my ancestors, and a humbling learning experience that has transformed me forever.

> *"Joy is her life's blood, spirit-food and soul-life all in one. Joy is the kind of feeling a woman has when she lays the words down on the paper just so, or hits the notes 'al punto', right on the head, the first time. Whew. Unbelievable. It is the kind of feeling a woman has when she finds she is pregnant and wants to be. It is the kind of joy a woman feels when she looks at people she loves enjoying themselves. It is the kind of joy a woman feels when she has done something that she feels dogged about, that she feels intense about, something that took risk, something that made her stretch, best herself, and succeed maybe gracefully, maybe not, but she did it, created the something, the someone, the art, the battle, the moment; her life. That is a woman's natural and instinctive state of being. Wild Woman emanates up through that kind of joy. That sort of soulful situation summons her by name."*
>
> —*Dr. Clarissa Pinkola Estés,* Women Who Run With the Wolves: Myths and Stories of the Wild Woman Archetype (240)

GLOSSARY

Burnout is a state of physical, emotional, and mental exhaustion caused by long-term involvement in emotionally demanding situations. Symptoms may include depression, cynicism, boredom, loss of compassion, and discouragement.

Compassion fatigue is a combination of physical, emotional, and spiritual depletion associated with caring for others who are in significant emotional pain and physical distress.

Compassion satisfaction refers to the pleasure derived from work, including feeling positively about the meaningfulness of one's contribution to the work and/or to the greater good of society.

Critical incident stress and traumatic stress are highly stressful situations, traumatic events, or perceived life-threatening events that have sufficient power to overwhelm an individual's ability to cope. Normal physical and psychological responses to the traumatic event occur, which place considerable pressure on that person. When the stressor becomes extremely threatening, overwhelming, or severe, it often produces a heightened state of cognitive, emotional, and behavioral arousal called traumatic stress. The terms "traumatic stress" and "critical incident stress" are often used interchangeably. After having been exposed to traumatic stress, individuals may

---

Happy Teacher Revolution gratefully acknowledges the U.S. Department of Justice, Office of Justice Programs, Office for Victims of Crime, for allowing us to reproduce in whole the *Vicarious Trauma Toolkit Glossary of Terms* (n.d.), a publication prepared by the Office for Victims of Crime.

experience a range of reactions immediately and/or over time, including decline in job performance, behavioral changes, anxiety, relationship discord, grief reactions, depression, and suicidal ideations.

Posttraumatic stress (PTS)/posttraumatic stress disorder (PTSD), as defined in the *Diagnostic and Statistical Manual of Mental Disorders, 5*, is a psychological reaction that occurs after experiencing a highly stressful event outside the range of normal human experience. PTS symptoms can happen without a full diagnosis of PTSD; the disorder is diagnosed when a number of the following PTS symptoms last longer than 1 month following a traumatic event:

- Re-experiencing or spontaneous memories and recurrent dreams of the traumatic event, flashbacks, or other intense or prolonged psychological distress.
- Avoidance of distressing memories, thoughts, feelings, or external reminders of the event.
- Negative cognitions and mood, including myriad feelings such as a persistent and distorted sense of blame of self or others, estrangement from others, markedly diminished interest in activities, and/or an inability to remember key aspects of the event.
- Arousal marked by aggressive, reckless, or self-destructive behavior; sleep disturbances; hypervigilance; and other related problems.

Resilience is the process of adapting well in the face of adversity, trauma, tragedy, threats, or significant sources of stress, such as family and relationship problems, serious health problems, or workplace and financial stressors.

Secondary traumatic stress (STS) refers to the natural consequent behaviors and emotions that often result from knowing about a traumatizing event experienced by another and the stress resulting from helping, or wanting to help, a traumatized or suffering person. Its symptoms can mimic those of posttraumatic stress disorder.

Traumatic stress is the stress response to a traumatic event of which one is a victim or witness. Repeated stressful or traumatic events can chronically elevate the body's stress response.

Vicarious resilience is a process of learning about overcoming adversity from a trauma survivor and the resulting positive transformation and empowerment experienced through witnessing the survivor's empathy and interaction.

Vicarious transformation is an ongoing, intentional process that results in a deepened sense of connection with others, a greater appreciation in one's life, and a greater sense of meaning and hope.

Vicarious trauma is an occupational challenge for people working and volunteering in fields with continuous or exposure to victims of trauma and violence. Exposure to the trauma of others has been shown to change the world-view of these responders and can put people and organizations at risk for a range of negative consequences.

Vicarious trauma-informed organizations proactively address the existence and impact of vicarious trauma on their staff through policies, procedures, practices, and programs that mitigate the risk of negative consequences for employees, the organization as a whole, and the quality of services delivered.

Vicarious traumatization is a *negative* reaction to trauma exposure and includes a range of psychosocial symptoms that providers and responders may experience through their intervention with those who are experiencing or have experienced trauma. It can include disruptions in thinking and changes in beliefs about one's sense of self, one's safety in the world, and the goodness and trustworthiness of others; as well as shifts in spiritual beliefs. Individuals may also exhibit symptoms that can have detrimental effects, both professionally and personally.

Victim service providers are professionals and volunteers who are trained to support victims/survivors of violence and other crimes by providing information, emotional support, resources, court advocacy and accompaniment, support groups, counseling, crisis hotlines, shelter, financial remedies, and other services in a trauma-informed, culturally relevant, and victim-centered manner. Victim service providers may work in government, criminal justice, nonprofit, or community-based organizations or agencies, among others. They may be referred to as victim advocates, victim/witness coordinators, rape crisis counselors, domestic violence advocates, victim counselors, victim/witness specialists, or protective workers, among other terms.

REFERENCES

Ackerman, Courtney. (2020). "What Is Happiness and Why Is It Important? (+ Definition in Psychology)." PositivePsychology.com, October 31. positivepsychology.com/what-is-happiness/

Aguilar, Elena. *Onward: Cultivating Emotional Resilience in Educators*. Jossey-Bass, 2018.

Amabile, Teresa M., and Steven J. Kramer. (2020). "The Power of Small Wins." *Harvard Business Review*, May 6. https://hbr.org/2011/05/the-power-of-small-wins

Auburn University Office of Inclusion and Diversity. (2022). "Thoughtful Thursdays." September 8. sustain.auburn.edu/event/thoughtful-thursdays/

Ayala, Erin E., et al. (2018). "U.S. Medical Students Who Engage in Self-Care Report Less Stress and Higher Quality of Life." *BMC Medical Education*, BioMed Central, August 6. www.ncbi.nlm.nih.gov/pmc/articles/PMC6080382/

Baas, Linda S., Theresa A. Beery, Gordon Allen, Michael Wizer, and Lynne E. Wagoner. (2004). "An Exploratory Study of Body Awareness in Persons with Heart Failure Treated Medically or with Transplantation." *Journal of Cardiovascular Nursing* 19 (1): 32–40.

Baird B., J. Smallwood, and J. W. Schooler. (2011). Back to the Future: Autobiographical Planning and the Functionality of Mind-Wandering. *Consciousness and Cognition* 20 (4). https://doi.org/10.1016/j.concog.2011.08.007

Banksy. (2021). "5 Best Banksy Quotes Worth Memorizing." Banksy: The Most Wanted Man in the World of Art (blog). January 30. https://banksybrooklyn.com/2021/01/30/5-best-banksy-quotes-worth-memorizing/

Baumeister, Roy F., and Mark R. Leary. (1995). "The Need to Belong: Desire for Interpersonal Attachments as a Fundamental Human Motivation." *Psychological Bulletin* 117 (3): 497–529. https://doi.org/10.1037/0033–2909.117.3.497

Beard, Alison. (2017). "Coach Mike Krzyzewski: To Recruit the Best, Tell the Truth about Who You Are." *Harvard Business Review*, February 21. hbr.org/2017/03/mike-krzyzewski

"Best Possible Self (Greater Good in Action)." (n.d.). Greater Good In Action, University of California, Berkeley. https://ggia.berkeley.edu/practice/best_possible_self

Bocchiaro, Piero, Philip G. Zimbardo, and Paul A. M. Van Lange. (2012). "To Defy or Not to Defy: An Experimental Study of the Dynamics of Disobedience and Whistle-Blowing," *Social Influence* 7:1, 35–50. doi: 10.1080/15534510.2011.648421

Brancatisano, Emma. (2016). "Why We Need to Learn to Sit with Discomfort." *HuffPost* Australia, November 3. https://www.huffpost.com/archive/au/entry/why-we-need-to-learn-to-sit-with-discomfort_au_5cd3790de4b0ce845d811e7e

Bronfenbrenner Center for Translational Research. (2019). "'Knowing Your Why' Is Good for You." *Psychology Today*, June 24. www.psychologytoday.com/us/blog/evidence-based-living/201906/knowing-your-why-is-good-you

brown, adrienne marie. (2021). *Holding Change: The Way of Emergent Strategy Facilitation and Mediation*. AK Press, Kindle Edition.

Brown, Brené. (2010a). *The Gifts of Imperfection: Let Go of Who You Think You Are Supposed to Be and Embrace Who You Are*. Hazelden. Kindle Edition.

Brown, Brené. (2010b). "The Power of Vulnerability." TEDxHouston, June. TED video, 20:03.

Brown, Brené. (2013). *Daring Greatly: How the Courage to Be Vulnerable Transforms the Way We Live, Love, Parent and Lead*. Portfolio Penguin.

Brown, Brené. (2015). "6 People Never to Trust with Your Secrets." *HuffPost*, March 12. https://www.huffpost.com/entry/brene-brown-shame_n_4282679

Brown, Brené. (2023). "Belonging + Self-Worth." *How She Really Does It Podcast*. Posted August 16, 2023. YouTube video, 1:08:59. https://www.youtube.com/watch?v=BMJCE-azS3Q

Brown, K. W., and R. M. Ryan. (2003). "The Benefits of Being Present: Mindfulness and Its Role in Psychological Well-Being. *Journal of Personality and Social Psychology* 84: 822–848.

Buettner, D., and S. Skemp. (2016). "Blue Zones: Lessons from the World's Longest Lived." *American Journal of Lifestyle Medicine* 10 (5): 318–321. doi.org/10. 1177/ 1559827616637066

Cabeen, Jessica M. (2023). *Principal in Balance Leading at Work and Living a Life*. Wiley.

Cacioppo J. T., and S. Cacioppo. (2014). "Older Adults Reporting Social Isolation or Loneliness Show Poorer Cognitive Function 4 Years Later." *Evidence-Based Nursing* 17 (2): 59–60. https://doi.org/10.1136/eb-2013–101379

Camera, Lauren. "International Survey: U.S. Teachers Are Overworked." US News, 19 June 2019, www.usnews.com/news/education-news/articles/2019-06-19/international-survey-us-teachers-are-overworked-feel-underappreciated

Cascio, C. N., et al. (2016). "Self-Affirmation Activates Brain Systems Associated with Self-Related Processing and Reward and Is Reinforced by Future Orientation." *Social Cognitive and Affective Neuroscience* 11 (4): 621–629. https://doi.org/10.1093/scan/nsv136

Cecelia, Jennae. (2020). *The Sun Will Rise and So Will We*. Self-published.

Ceci, M. W., and V. K. Kumar. (2016). "A Correlational Study of Creativity, Happiness, Motivation, and Stress from Creative Pursuits." *Journal of Happiness Studies* 17: 609–626. https://doi.org/10.1007/s10902–015–9615-y

Chödrön, Pema. (n.d.). "7 Life Lessons from Pema Chödrön." *Guided Mind*. Accessed October 30, 2023. https://www.guidedmind.com/blog/7-life-lessons-from-pema-chodron

Church, C., O. A. Andreassen, S. Lorentzen, I. Melle, and M. Aas. (2017). "Childhood Trauma and Minimization/Denial in People with and without a Severe Mental Disorder." *Frontiers in Psychology* 8: 1276. https://doi.org/10.3389/fpsyg.2017.01276

Clark, David. (2018). "Bessel van Der Kolk: The Importance of Safety and Reciprocity." *Sharing Culture*, Apr. 24. sharingculture.info/davids-blog/bessel-van-der-kolk-the-importance-of-safety-and-reciprocity#:~:text=The%20critical%20issue%20is%20reciprocity,a%20visceral%20feeling%20of%20safety

Clay, Valencia D. (2016). *Soundless Cries Don't Lead to Healing: A Critical Thinking Guide to Cultural Consciousness.* Ingram-Spark.

Clay-Bell, Valencia D. (2023). *Grow Beyond Creative Barriers G.R.O.W. Productivity Guide: 100 Self-Paced Strategies.* Fabian Bell.

Clear Sky Children's Charity. (2023). *Clear Sky: The Power of Play,* July 6. clear-sky.org.uk/

Cohen, Geoffrey. (2022). *Belonging the Science of Creating Connection and Bridging Divides.* Norton.

Cordeiro, P. M. G., M. P. Paixão, W. Lens, and K. Sheldon. (2016). "Factor Structure and Dimensionality of the Balanced Measure of Basic Psychological Needs among Portuguese High School Students. Relations to Well-Being and Ill-Being." *Learning and Individual Differences* 47:51–60. https://doi.org/10.1016/j.lindif.2015.12.010

Costa, Christina. (2021). *Kiss Your Brain: Diagnosis Diaries.* Self-published.

Coster, J. S., and M. Schwebel. (1997). "Well-Functioning in Professional Psychologists." *Professional Psychology: Research and Practice* 28 (1): 5–13. https://doi.org/10.1037/0735-7028.28.1.5

Cropley, Mark, Derk-Jan Dijk, and Neil Stanley (2006). "Job Strain, Work Rumination, and Sleep in School Teachers." *European Journal of Work and Organizational Psychology* 15 (2): 181–196. https://doi.org/10.1080/13594320500513913

Dana, Deb. (2021). *Anchored: How to Befriend Your Nervous System Using Polyvagal Theory.* Sounds True. Kindle edition.

Darley, John M., and Bibb Latané. (1968). "Bystander Intervention in Emergencies: Diffusion of Responsibility." *Journal of Personality and Social Psychology* 8 (4): 377–383.

Darling-Hammond, Linda, Roberta Furger, Patrick Shields, and Leib Sutcher. (2016). "Addressing California's Emerging Teacher Shortage: An Analysis of Sources and Solutions." Learning Policy Institute. www.learningpolicyinstitute.org/addressing-ca-teacher-shortage

Daulat, Neesha Y. (2020). "Reinforcing Early Career Teachers' Sense of Purpose: A Mechanism to Sustain Early Career Teachers in the Profession." Claremont Graduate University. June 5.

Davis, Vicki. (2014). "12 Choices to Help You Step Back from Burnout." *Edutopia,* May 20. www.edutopia.org/blog/12-choices-step-back-from-burnout-vicki-davis

Dolan, Simon, Ben Capell, Shay Tzafrir, and Guy Enosh. (2014). "Disclosure of Stigmatized Identity: The Role of Trust." Presented at the 30th EGOS Colloquium. https://www.researchgate.net/publication/279922085_Disclosure_of_Stigmatized_Identity_The_Role_of_Trust

Dore, Jessica. (2021). *Tarot for Change: Using the Cards for Self-Care, Acceptance and Growth.* Hay House.

Duman, Ronald S. (2004). "Neural Plasticity: Consequences of Stress and Actions of Antidepressant Treatment." *Dialogues in Clinical Neuroscience* 6(2): 157–169.

Education Now News Editor. (2022). "Navigating Trauma—for Teachers and Learners." Harvard Graduate School of Education. April 20. https://www.gse.harvard.edu/ideas/education-now/22/04/navigating-trauma-teachers-and-learners

Emdin, Christopher. (2016). *For White Folks Who Teach in the Hood . . . and the Rest of Y'all Too: Reality Pedagogy and Urban Education.* Beacon Press. Kindle Edition.

Emdin, Christopher. (2021). *Ratchetdemic: Reimagining Academic Success.* Beacon Press. Kindle Edition.

Emdin, Christopher (@chrisemdin). (2020). "An Educator Who Feels Unsafe, Uncared for & Devalued Cannot Give Their Full Selves to their work. Basic human needs extend to Those who Teach as Much as They Do to Those who Are to Be Taught." Twitter, July 3, 2020, 11:30 a.m. https://twitter.com/chrisemdin/status/1279120375037788160?lang=en

Emerson, Michelle. (2023). *First-Class Teaching: 10 Lessons You Don't Learn in College.* Jossey-Bass.

Emmons, R., and C. Shelton. (2002). "Gratitude and the Science of Positive Psychology." In *Handbook of Positive Psychology,* ed. C. R. Snyder and Shane J. Lopez, pp. 459–471. Oxford University Press.

Estés, Clarissa Pinkola. (2003). *Women Who Run with the Wolves: Myths and Stories of the Wild Woman Archetype.* Ballantine Books.

Firestone, Lisa. (2017). "The Unselfish Art of Prioritizing Yourself." *Psychology Today,* August 17. www.psychologytoday.com/us/blog/compassion-matters/201708/the-unselfish-art-prioritizing-yourself

Flett, Alison L., Mohsen Haghbin, and Timothy A. Pychyl. (2016). "Procrastination and Depression from a Cognitive Perspective: An Exploration of the Associations among Procrastinatory Automatic Thoughts, Rumination, and Mindfulness." *Journal of Rational-Emotive & Cognitive-Behavior Therapy* 34: 169–186. https://doi.org/10.1007/s10942–016–0235–1

Ford, J. D., and C. A. Courtois, eds. (2013). *Treating Complex Trauma Stress Disorders in Children and Adolescents: Scientific Foundations and Therapeutic Models.* Guilford Press.

Fotiadis A., K. Abdulrahman, and A. Spyridou. (2019). "The Mediating Roles of Psychological Autonomy, Competence and Relatedness on Work-Life Balance and Well-Being." *Frontiers in Psychology* 10: 1267. https://doi.org/10.3389/fpsyg.2019.01267

Frenzel A. C., et al. (2016). Measuring Teachers' Enjoyment, Anger, and Anxiety: The Teacher Emotions Scales (TES). *Contemporary Educational Psychology* 46: 148–163.

Gaffney, Carrie. (2019). "When Schools Cause Trauma." *Learning for Justice* 62. www.learningforjustice.org/magazine/summer-2019/when-schools-cause-trauma

Gomes, Carol. (n.d.). "Code Lavender—Caring for Our Caregivers." Stony Brook Medicine. Accessed October 30, 2023. www.stonybrookmedicine.edu/code_lavender_caring_for_our_caregivers

Gomez, Daphne. (2022). "Stress Is Pushing Many Teachers Out of the Profession." *Forbes,* February 23. https://www.forbes.com/sites/forbescoachescouncil/2022/02/23/stress-is-pushing-many-teachers-out-of-the-profession/?sh=4ca53666942b

Goodman, Whitney. (2022). *Toxic Positivity: Keeping It Real in a World Obsessed with Being Happy.* TarcherPerigee, Penguin Random House.

Goodman, Whitney. (2023). "The Art of Complaining: Eight Tips to Finesse It and Actually Make Things Happen." *Australian Women's Weekly,* July 22. www.womensweekly.com.au/health/wellness/how-to-complain- effectively-74902/

Graves, Justin. (2020). "Hesonwheels.Com," January 8. hesonwheels.com/

Gray, Rosie. "Teachers in America Were Already Facing Collapse. Covid Only Made It Worse." BuzzFeed News, BuzzFeed News, 1 Apr. 2022, www.buzzfeednews.com/article/rosiegray/america-teaching-collapse-covid-education.

Greene, Amy. "Code Lavender." Code Lavender, Mar. 2019, info.5y1.org/tampa-general-medical-group-medical-records_2_4eac6a.html.

Herrero, Jose L., Simon Khuvis, Erin Yeagle, Moran Cerf, and Ashesh D. Mehta. (2018). "Breathing above the Brain Stem: Volitional Control and Attentional Modulation in Humans." *Journal of Neurophysiology* 119 (1): 145–159. https://doi.org/10.1152/jn.00551.2017

Hersey, Tricia. (2022). *Rest Is Resistance: A Manifesto.* Little, Brown Spark.

Holt-Lunstad, J., T. B. Smith, and J. B. Layton (2010). "Social Relationships and Mortality Risk: A Meta-Analytic Review." *PLos Medicine* 7 (7): 4. https://doi.org/10.1371/journal.pmed.1000316

Huang, L. N., et al. (2014). SAMHSA's Concept of Trauma and Guidance for a Trauma-Informed Approach (SMA No. 14-4884). https://store.samhsa.gov/product/SAMHSA-s-Concept-of-Trauma-and-Guidance-for-a-Trauma-Informed-Approach/SMA14–4884

Huo, Yuanyuan, Wing Lam, and Ziguang Chen. (2012). "Am I the Only One This Supervisor Is Laughing At? Effects of Aggressive Humor on Employee Strain and Addictive Behaviors." *Personnel Psychology* 65 (4): 859–885.

Itzchakov, Guy, and Avraham N. Kluger. (2018.) "The Power of Listening in Helping People Change." *Harvard Business Review*, May 17. hbr.org/2018/05/the-power-of-listening-in-helping-people-change

Jennings, P. A., and Greenberg, M. T. (2009). "The Prosocial Classroom: Teacher Social and Emotional Competence in Relation to Student and Classroom Outcomes." *Review of Educational Research* 79: 491–525.

Jennings, Patricia A. (2015a). *Mindfulness for Teachers: Simple Skills for Peace and Productivity in the Classroom.* Norton.

Jennings, Patricia. (2015b). "Seven Ways Mindfulness Can Help Teachers." *Greater Good*, March 30. greatergood.berkeley.edu/article/item/seven_ways_mindfulness_can_help_teachers

Jewell, Tiffany. (2020). *This Book Is Anti-Racist: 20 Lessons on How to Wake Up, Take Action, and Do the Work.* Quarto Publishing Group.

Johnson, Kimberly Ann. (2021.) *Call of the Wild: How We Heal Trauma, Awaken Our Own Power, and Use It for Good.* HarperCollins.

Johnson, Mona M. (2002). *Making Professional Wellness a Priority!* https://rems.ed.gov/docs/RSE%20TtT%20Participant%20Workbook%202020.pdf https://education.mn.gov/mdeprod/idcplg?IdcService=GET_FILE&dDocName=PROD046212&RevisionSelectionMethod=latestReleased&Rendition=primary

Kamenetz, Anya."More than Half of Teachers Are Looking for the Exits, a Poll Says." NPR, NPR, 1 Feb. 2022, www.npr.org/2022/02/01/1076943883/teachers-quitting-burnout.

Kim-Prieto, Chu, Ed Diener, Maya Tamir, Christie N. Scollon, and Marrisa Diener. (2005). "Integrating the Diverse Definitions of Happiness: A Time-Sequential Framework of Subjective Well-Being." *Journal of Happiness Studies* 6 (3): 261–300.

King, Laura, and Jeffrey Huffman. (n.d.). "Best Possible Self." Greater Good in Action, Greater Good Science Center. Accessed 18 Dec. 2023. ggia.berkeley.edu/practice/practice_as_pdf/best_possible_self?printPractice=Y#:~:text=This%20exercise%20asks%20you%20to,sustained%20happiness%20down%20the%20line

Kirsch, Nancy. (n.d. [2021]). "It's Not Burnout! It is Moral Injury: Why Should Regulators be Concerned?" www.fsbpt.org/Free-Resources/FSBPT-Forum/Forum-2021/Its-Not-Burnout-It-is-Moral-Injury-Why-Should-Regulators-be-Concerned

Klein, Alyson. "Superficial Self-Care? Stressed-out Teachers Say No Thanks." Education Week, Education Week, 9 June 2022, www.edweek.org/teaching-learning/superficial-self-care-stressed-out-teachers-say-no-thanks/2022/03.

Kleinrock, Liz. (2021). *Start Here Start Now: A Guide to Anti Bias and Antiracist Work in Your Community*. Heinemann.

Koenig, Harold G., and Faten Al Zaben. (2021). "Moral Injury: An Increasingly Recognized and Widespread Syndrome." *Journal of Religion and Health* 60 (5): 2989–3011. https://doi.org/10.1007/s10943-021-01328-0

Kovess-Masféty, V., C. Sevilla-Dedieu, C. Rios-Seidel, E. Nerrière, and C. Chan Chee. (2006). "Do Teachers Have More Health Problems? Results from a French Cross-Sectional Survey." *BMC Public Health* 6: 101. https://bmcpublichealth.biomedcentral.com/articles/10.1186/1471-2458-6-101

Kowalski, Robin M., et al. (2014). "Pet Peeves and Happiness: How do Happy People Complain?" *Journal of Social Psychology* 154 (4): 278–282. https://doi.org/10.1080/00224545.2014.906380

Krasnoff, Basha. (2017). "A Practitioner's Guide to Educating Traumatized Children." *Education Northwest*, p. 6–7. https://educationnorthwest.org/resources/practitioners-guide-educating-traumatized-children

Langan-Fox, Janice, Cary L. Cooper, and Richard J. Klimoski, eds. (2007). *Research Companion to the Dysfunctional Workplace: Management Challenges and Symptoms*. Edward Elgar.

Lewandowski, G. R., N. Nardon, and A. J. Raines. (2010). "The Role of Self-Concept Clarity in Relationship Quality." *Self and Identity* 9 (4): 416–433. https://www.researchgate.net/publication/233377858_The_Role_of_Self-concept_Clarity_in_Relationship_Quality

Lu, Stacy (2015). "Mindfulness Holds Promise for Treating Depression." *Monitor on Psychology* 46 (3): 50. http://www.apa.org/monitor/2015/03/cover-mindfulness

Lyall, Laura M., et al. (2018). "Association of Disrupted Circadian Rhythmicity with Mood Disorders, Subjective Well-Being, and Cognitive Function: A Cross-Sectional Study of 91,105 Participants from the UK Biobank." *Lancet Psychiatry* 5 (6): 507–514. https://doi.org/10.1016/S2215–0366(18)30139–1

Magnus-Sharpe, Sarah. (2022). "Leaving Your Comfort Zone Inspires Motivation, Growth." *Cornell Chronicle*, March 29. https://news.cornell.edu/stories/2022/03/leaving-your-comfort-zone-inspires-motivation-growth

Maslach, C., S. E. Jackson, and M. P. Leiter. (1996). *Maslach Burnout Inventory*. Consulting Psychologists Press.

Maslach, C., W. B. Schaufeli, and M. P. Leiter. (2001). "Job Burnout." *Annual Review of Psychology* 52: 397–422. https://www.annualreviews.org/doi/abs/10.1146/annurev.psych.52.1.397

Maslach, Christina, and Mary Gomes. (2006). "Overcoming Burnout." In *Working for Peace: A Handbook of Practical Psychology and Other Tools*, ed. Rachel McNair and Psychologists for Social Responsibility, 43–36. Impact.

McLean, L., and C. M. Connor. (2015). "Depressive Symptoms in Third Grade Teachers: Relations to Classroom Quality and Student Achievement." *Child Development* 86: 945–954. https://www.ncbi.nlm.nih.gov/pmc/articles/PMC4428950/

Mehling, Wolf E., et al. (2009). "Body Awareness: Construct and Self-Report Measures." *PLos ONE* 4 (5): e5614. https://doi.org/10.1371/journal.pone.0005614

Mertoğlu, Münevver. (2018). "Happiness Level of Teachers and Analyzing Its Relation with Some Variables." *Asian Journal of Education and Training* 4 (4): 374–380. https://doi.org/10.20448/journal.522.2018.44.396.402

Montgomery, C., and A. A. Rupp. (2005). "A Meta-Analysis Exploring the Diverse Causes and Effects of Stress in Teachers." *Canadian Journal of Education* 28 (3): 458–486. https://doi.org/10.2307/4126479

Myers, Lindsay. (2014). "The Self-Help Industry Helps Itself to Billions of Dollars." Brain Blogger. www.brainblogger.com/2014/05/23/the-self-help-industry-helps-itself-to-billions-of-dollars/

Nagoski, Emily, and Amelia Nagoski. (2020). *Burnout: The Secret to Unlocking the Stress Cycle.* Ballantine Books.

National Center for Education Statistics, US Department of Education. (2022). Table 208.20. Public and Private Elementary and Secondary Teachers, Enrollment, Pupil/Teacher Ratios, and New Teacher Hires: Selected Years, Fall 1955 through Fall 2031. 2022 Tables and Figures. *Digest of Education Statistics.* https://nces.ed.gov/programs/digest/d20/tables/dt20_208.20.asp

National Commission on Teaching and America's Future. (n.d. [2015]). "Policy Brief: The High Cost of Teacher Turnover." https://nieer.org/wp-content/uploads/2015/06/NCTAF-CostofTeacherTurnoverpolicybrief.pdf

National Education Association. (2022). Policy Statements 2021–2022." January. www.nea.org/sites/default/files/2022-06/NEA%20Policy%20Statements%202021-2022.pdf

National Institute of Standards and Technology. (2021). "Human Centered Design (HCD)." May 3, 2021. www.nist.gov/itl/iad/visualization-and-usability-group/human-factors-human-centered-design

Neff, Kristin D., and Andrew P. Costigan. (2014). "Self-Compassion, Well-Being, and Happiness." *Psychologie in Osterreich* 2 (3): 114–117. https://self-compassion.org/wp-content/uploads/publications/Neff&Costigan.pdf

O'Brien, Maryanne. (2021). *The Elevated Communicator: How to Master Your Style and Strengthen Well-Being at Work.* Simon Element.

Odell, Jenny. (2021). *How to Do Nothing: Resisting the Attention Economy.* Melville House.

Office for Victims of Crime. (n.d.) "The Vicarious Trauma Toolkit: Glossary of Terms." US Department of Justice, Office of Justice Programs. Accessed July 24, 2023. https://ovc.ojp.gov/program/vtt/glossary-terms#glossary-of-terms

Orr, Gregory. (2002). *Poetry as Survival.* University of Georgia.

Patterson, Lyn. "Nothing on the Internet Ever Dies". Self Published, Lyn Patterson, 2020.

Pathan, Nazima. (2018). "Procrastination: It's Pretty Much All in the Mind." *BBC News,* August 26. www.bbc.com/news/health-45295392

Perry, Bruce, and Oprah Winfrey. (2021). *What Happened to You?: Conversations on Trauma, Resilience, and Healing.* Bluebird. Kindle Edition.

Pitterson, N., C. Allendoerfer, R. Streveler, J. Ortega-Alvarez, and K. Smith. (2020). "The Importance of Community in Fostering Change: A Qualitative Case Study of the Rigorous Research in Engineering Education (RREE) Program." *Studies in Engineering Education* 1 (1): 20–37. https://doi.org/http://doi.org/10.21061/see.7

Plyler, Jen. (2009). "How to Keep on Keeping On." *Upping the Anti* 3: 123–134. https://uppingtheanti.org/journal/article/03-how-to-keep-on-keeping-on/

Podolsky, A., T. Kini, and L. Darling-Hammond. (2019). "Does Teaching Experience Increase Teacher Effectiveness? A Review of US Research," *Journal of Professional Capital and Community* 4(4): 286–308. https://doi.org/10.1108/JPCC-12-2018-0032

Policy Brief: The High Cost of Teacher Turnover. Retrieved from http://nctaf.org/wp-content/uploads/2012/01/NCTAF-Cost-of-Teacher-Turnover2007-policy-brief.pdf

Price, C. J. and C. Hooven. (2018). "Interoceptive Awareness Skills for Emotion Regulation: Theory and Approach of Mindful Awareness in Body-Oriented Therapy (MABT)." *Frontiers in Psychology* 9: 798. doi: 10.3389/fpsyg.2018.00798. PMID: 29892247; PMCID: PMC5985305

Rankin, Jenny Grant. (2017). *First Aid for Teacher Burnout: Helping Current and Aspiring Teachers Craving Peace and Success.* Routledge. Kindle Edition.

Rennis, Lesley, Gloria McNamara, Erica Seidel and Yuliya Shneyderman. (2014). "Google It!: Urban Community College Students' Use of the Internet to Obtain Self-Care and Personal Health Information." *College Student Journal,* Project Innovation, 49(3): 414–426. https://www.researchgate.net/publication/266812579_Google_It_Urban_community_college_student_use_of_the_internet_to_obtain_self-care_and_personal_health_information

Rettig, Hilary. (2006). *The Lifelong Activist: How to Change the World Without Losing Your Way.* Lantern.

Richards, Kelly, C. Estelle Campenni, and Janet L. Muse-Burke. (2010). "Self-Care and Well-Being in Mental Health Professionals: The Mediating Effects of Self-Awareness and Mindfulness." *Journal of Mental Health Counseling* 32 (3): 247–264. https://doi.org/10.17744/mehc.32.3.0n31v88304423806

Ritchie, T. D., C. Sedikides, T. Wildschut, J. Arndt, and Y. Gidron. (2011). "Self-Concept Clarity Mediates the Relation Between Stress and Subjective Well-Being. *Self and Identity* 10 (4): 493–508. https://doi.org/10.1080/15298868.2010.493066

Robins, Ellie. (2017). "The Secret Benefit of Routines. It Won't Surprise You." *Headspace,* July 19. www.headspace.com/blog/2016/08/22/the-secret-benefit-of-routines-it-wont-surprise-you/

Rock, David, and Christine Cox. "SCARF® in 2012: Updating the Social Neuroscience of Collaborating with Others." *NeuroLeadership Journal,* no. 4. https://www.academia.edu/25000956/SCARF_in_2012_updating_the_social_neuroscience_of_collaborating_with_others

Róisín, Fariha. (2022). *Who is Wellness For? An Examination of Wellness Culture and Who It Leaves Behind.* New York: HarperCollins. Kindle Edition.

Rolls, E. T., M. L. Kringelbach, and I. E. T. Araujo. (2003). "Different Representations of Pleasant and Unpleasant Odors in the Human Brain." *European Journal of Neuroscience* 18 (3): 695–703. https://doi.org/10.1046/j.1460–9568.2003.02779.x

Ronfeldt, M., S. Loeb, and J. Wyckoff. (2013). "How Teacher Turnover Harms Student Achievement." *American Educational Research Journal* 50 (1): 4–36. https://doi.org/10.3102/0002831212463813

Rothstein, Lori, and Denise Stromme. (n.d.) "Celebrate the Small Stuff." Episode 4.1. Two for You Series. University of Minnesota Extension. Accessed July 11, 2023. extension.umn.edu/two-you-video-series/celebrate-small-stuff

Ryff, Carol D., and Keyes, C. (1995). "The structure of psychological well-being revisited." *Journal of Personality and Social Psychology* 69: 719–727. https://doi.org/10.1037//0022-3514.69.4.719.

Salzberg, Sharon. (2004). *Lovingkindness: The Revolutionary Art of Happiness.* Boulder, CO: Shambhala. Kindle Edition.

Schmidt, Brie. (2023). "TikTok's 'Filler Episode' Days Are More Than a Trend: They're the Reprieve You Need." *Glam,* May 21. www.glam.com/1292052/tiktok-filler-episode-days-mental-health-benefits/

Seifert, Tricia. (2018.) "The Ryff Scales of Psychological Well-Being." Center of Inquiry at Wabash College. centerofinquiry.org/uncategorized/ryff-scales-of-psychological-well-being/

Smith, David, and Nicky Woolf. (2016). "Democrats Continue House Sit-in Demanding Vote on Gun Control." *The Guardian,* June 22. https://www.theguardian.com/us-news/2016/jun/22/house-democrats-stage-sit-vote-gun-control

Sparks, Sarah D. "Teachers' Pay Lags Furthest behind Other Professionals in U.S., Study Finds." Education Week, Education Week, 17 Sept. 2017, www.edweek.org/policy-politics/teachers-pay-lags-furthest-behind-other-professionals-in-u-s-study-finds/2017/09.

Stark, K., N. Daulat, and S. King. (2022). A Vision for Teachers' Emotional Well-Being. *Phi Delta Kappan* 103 (5). https://doi.org/10.1177/00317217221079975

Study International Staff. (2018) "The Science behind Procrastination and How to Overcome It." *Study International,* September 27. www.studyinternational.com/news/the-science-behind-procrastination-and-how-to-overcome-it/

Svoboda, Elizabeth. (2019). "How to Stand up for What's Right, Even If You're Afraid." *Greater Good,* October 17, 2019. https://greatergood.berkeley.edu/article/item/how_to_stand_up_for_whats_right_even_if_youre_afraid

Taren, Adrienne A., et al. (2015). "Mindfulness Meditation Training Alters Stress-Related Amygdala Resting State Functional Connectivity: A Randomized Controlled Trial." *Social Cognitive and Affective Neuroscience* 10 (12): 1758–1768. https://doi.org/10.1093/scan/nsv066

Tawwab, Nedra Glover. (2021). *Set Boundaries, Find Peace: A Guide to Reclaiming Yourself.* TarcherPerigee. Kindle Edition.

Tepper, Bennett J., et al. (2009). "Abusive Supervision, Intentions to Quit, and Employees' Workplace Deviance: A Power/Dependence Analysis." *Organizational Behavior and Human Decision Processes* 109 (2): 156–157. https://doi.org/10.1016/j.obhdp.2009.03.004

Tutu, Desmond. Desmond Tutu Quote, www.azquotes.com/quote/529521. Accessed 11 Mar. 2024.

Turner, Toko-pa. (2021). *Belonging: Remembering Ourselves Home*. Rider. Kindle Edition.

Tuxford L.M., and G. L. Bradley. (2015). "Emotional Job Demands and Emotional Exhaustion in Teachers." *Educational Psychology* 35 (8): 1006–1024.

Van der Kolk, Bessel. (2015). *The Body Keeps the Score: Mind, Brain and Body in the Transformation of Trauma*. Penguin Books. Kindle Edition.

Walker, Alice. (1989). *The Temple of My Familiar*. Harcourt.

Weissberg R. P., Durlak J. A., Domitrovich C. E., Gullotta T. P. (2015). *Social and emotional learning: Past, present, and future*. In Durlak J. A., Domitrovich C. E., Weissberg R. P., Gullotta T. P. (Eds.), *Handbook of social and emotional learning: Research and practice* (pp. 3–19). New York, NY: Guilford.

Will, Madeline. "Educators Are More Stressed at Work than Average People, Survey Finds." Education Week, Education Week, 30 Oct. 2017, www.edweek.org/teaching-learning/educators-are-more-stressed-at-work-than-average-people-survey-finds/2017/10.

Will, Madeline. "Teachers Are Not Ok, Even Though We Need Them to Be." Education Week, Education Week, 14 September 2021, www.edweek.org/teaching-learning/teachers-are-not-ok-even-though-we-need-them-to-be/2021/09.

Will, Madeline. (2020). "A Third of Teachers Are at Higher Risk of Severe Illness from COVID-19." *Education Week: Teaching Now*. blogs.edweek.org/teachers/teaching_now/2020/04/a_third_of_teachers_are_at_higher_risk_of_severe_illness_from_covid-19.html

Will, Madeline. (2022). "Teachers Are Not OK, Even Though We Need Them to Be." *Education Week, Education Week*, June 2, 2022. https://www.edweek.org/teaching-learning/teachers-are-not-ok-even-though-we-need-them-to-be/2021/09?utm_source=nl&utm_medium=eml&utm_campaign=eu&M=63883822&U=1616439&UUID=960abd1660cf6c723e361bd70e92ce5f.

Will, Madeline. "Violence, Threats, and Harassment Are Taking a Toll on Teachers, Survey Shows." Education Week, Education Week, 17 Mar. 2022, www.edweek.org/leadership/violence-threats-and-harassment-are-taking-a-toll-on-teachers-survey-shows/2022/03.

Williams, Mary Elizabeth. (2017). "Why Every Mind Needs Mindfulness," *Mindfulness: The New Science of Health and Happiness. TIME*, December 15, 9–15.

Willis, Judy. (2014). "Teacher's Guide to Sleep: and Why It Matters." *The Guardian*, November 11, 2014. www.theguardian.com/teacher-network/teacher-blog/2014/nov/11/good-night-teacher-guide-sleep

Wineman, Steve (2003). Power-Under: Trauma and Nonviolent Social Change. Self-published. http://www.traumaandnonviolence.com/

Wood, Stephen, and Lilian M. de Menezes. (2011). "High Involvement Management, High-Performance Work Systems and Well-Being." *International Journal of Human Resource Management* 22 (7). https://doi.org/10.1080/09585192.2011.561967

Woolley, K., and A. Fishbach. (2022). "Motivating Personal Growth by Seeking Discomfort." *Psychological Science* 33 (4): 510–523. https://doi.org/10.1177/09567976211044685

Wray-Lake, L., L. Halgunseth, and D. P. Witherspoon. (2022) "Good Trouble, Necessary Trouble: Expanding Thinking and Research on Youth of Color's Resistance to Oppression." *Journal of Research on Adolescence* 32 (2): 949–958. https://onlinelibrary.wiley.com/doi/abs/10.1111/jora.12773

INDEX